RETRO
DESSERTS

RETRO

LUSCIOUS CAKES

DESSERTS

TOTALLY HIP, UPDATED CLASSIC DESSERTS

from the '40s, '50s, '60s, *and* '70s

SWELL!

Wayne Harley Brachman

Photography by Dennis M. Gottlieb

William Morrow

An Imprint of HarperCollinsPublishers

FIRST EDITION

Designed by Leah Carlson-Stanisic
Photography by Dennis M. Gottlieb
Prop styling by Wayne Harley Brachman and Dennis M.Gottlieb
Food styling by Elizabeth Duffy

Library of Congress Cataloging-in-Publication Data
    Brachman, Wayne Harley.
     Retro desserts: totally hip, updated classic desserts from the '40s,
  '50s, '60s, and '70s / Wayne Harley Brachman ;
  photography by Dennis M. Gottlieb.—1st ed.
     p.   cm.
    Includes index.
    ISBN 0-688-16444-7
    1. Desserts. I. Title.
    TX773.B69724   2000
    641.8'621—dc21   99–043578

01 02 03 04 QKH 10 9 8 7 6 5 4 3

FOR *Isabella*

YOUR GRANDMA SYLVIA COULD HARDLY BOIL AN EGG
BUT SHE SURE COULD CRACK A JOKE

C O N T

ENTS

ACKNOWLEDGMENTS

Thanks for the help. Thanks for the memories. Most of all, thanks to the following: First off, the magnificent team at William Morrow. Justin Schwartz is the editor meister. Man, does this guy work it out. And, he occasionally thinks that I make sense. His talented assistant, Elena Wiesenthal, makes mincemeat of dirty work. Art director Leah Carlson-Stanisic gives the phrase "right on" a whole new meaning. Carrie Weinberg, publicist magnifique, did I ever tell you that you are fabulous?

Jane Dystel is the most wonderful agent and friend an author could have.

For those who don't know, photographer Dennis Gottlieb and I were separated at birth. But seriously, folks, can this guy click a camera or what? Dennis, you are the Lord of the Shutterbugs. Elizabeth Duffy, your plates look divine. My wife, Jacqueline, and my brother, Gerry, thanks for schlepping to the flea markets to help me find plates and props.

Pastry chefs are all jealous of the amazingly talented and dedicated staff who work for me. Their ideas, support, and assistance with the recipes were invaluable. And how do they manage to endure my corny jokes . . . day after day after day? Hats off to Virginia Ng of Bolo, Amanda Longo of Mesa Grill, and extra special thanks to my right-hand man, Alfred Stephens. Thanks to Mesa alumni Joe Oliviera, Jeremy Stoller, and Gail Morales.

Thank you so, so much, Jennifer Birnbach of Nickelodeon. Your efforts helped to create the "Desserts on the Dial" sections.

I work for a wonderful and supportive group of people: Laurence Kretchmer, Jerry Kretchmer, Dorothy Kretchmer, and my mentor and good buddy, Bobby Flay.

Saving the best for last, and let me tell you, she is the best. Stephanie Banyas, you are the ginchiest. You pointed out the direction for this book from the very beginning.

RETRO DESSERTS

INTRODUCTION

Culinary Memorabilia—All Natural—Slow Food—Fast and Snappy Recipes—No Instant Anything

These are the classics, clones, modern-day versions and composites of the camp and kitsch favorites that we all remember. We made them in home economics class, bought them at the grocery store, and brought them home from the supermarket. We read the ads, sang the jingles, and saw the commercials. These recipes contain no artificial ingredients. They require no instant this or instant that. Everything in this book is made from scratch. Now you can make your favorite desserts of the past.

Kitsch Desserts for Today's Kitchens

The recipes in this book were formulated from hundreds of authentic period recipes that were collected in vintage magazines, books, and advertisements. Several of them are composites of originals. In a few cases they are actually retro fakes. Which ones? you ask. Well, did Gimbel's tell Macy's?

LEARN TO BAKE—
You'll love it!

Someone Left the Cake Out in the Rain . . .

The tiki lamps swayed in the breeze, casting Technicolor flecks across the kidney-shaped swimming pool and flagstone patio. The guests, satiated on tuna casserole, pigs-in-a-blanket, and heaven knows how many whiskey sours, swayed to the lilting rhythms of Guy Lombardo & His Royal Canadians. They were playing a swinging cover of "Volare." But, this was just a prelude. This was just an overture. Suddenly, Dad deserted his post at the limbo pole, ripped off his "Come 'n' Get It" apron, and dashed to the hi-fi. With a scratch and a thud, he flipped on his brand-new album: *The Champagne Magic of Lawrence Welk.* Imaginary bubbles filled the knotty-pine den and, with a rustle of taffeta, Mom made her grand entrance. She had the effervescence of Doris Day, the grace of Loretta Young, the glamour of Gina Lollobrigida, and . . . the cake of Betty Crocker! It was pink. It was fluffy. It was voluptuous. It didn't taste quite as good as it looked.

For desserts, it was the best of times and the worst of times. It was that goofy period from World War II to the American food revolution of the late seventies, when culinary style was controlled by hordes of button-down ad execs on Madison Avenue. It was also the dawn of conspicuous consumption. Vance Packard complained that American TV was a vast wasteland. Television commercials packed America's vast waistlines with scarce a complaint.

Homemakers suddenly had more time for leisure, and their appetites were whetted for more. The door was opened for the mass marketing of quick new cooking methods and convenience foods.

America has always been the land of plenty, and plenty of opportunity: Any kid can grow up to be president. Any insurance actuary can make important medical decisions and any basketball player can get paid millions to make a deodorant commercial. Most countries have spent long, hard times, when mommies and *grand-mères* toiled in their kitchens to get the most out of meager ingredients. Here it was different. In the fifties, product development departments and advertising agencies became the major sources of recipe development. A lot was stupid. Every now and then, they came up with some pretty good stuff.

A beautiful cake is a joy forever, so take care. It can take a very long time to make it and you may never have that recipe again!

Before You Start

NUTS ✦ *For More Flavor, Make Them the TOAST of the Town.*
Calling all nut lovers, nutcases, and plain old nuts . . .
Flavorful things happen when nuts are toasted. They become crisp, crunchy, and flavorful. It's what we recommend in all of our recipes. So try nut toasting—it's as easy as 1–2–3.

1. Spread the nuts on a cookie sheet. Place in a preheated 325°F oven for 3 minutes or 2 minutes for coconut flakes.
2. For even toasting, turn the tray, front to back. Toss the nuts with a metal spatula and bake for another 3 minutes.
3. Sniff, sniff . . . Your nuts will tell you when they are ready with their fragrant aroma. And remember: Every oven is slightly different, so check your nuts. Don't ever let them become overbaked or charred.

COCONUT ✦ *Well, this is a lovely bunch of coconuts.*
Unsweetened coconut is available in health food stores and oriental groceries. If you can't find unsweetened coconut, you can either rinse the sweetened stuff in a colander under cold running water or subtract 2 tablespoons of sugar from the recipe.

EGGS ✦ *The Russians Are Coming . . . in Flying Saucers!*
In the fifties, Americans feared imminent annihilation at the hands of Martians and/or Communists. Today we've got the very real dangers of salmonella, plus all sorts of new allergies and talk-show hosts to threaten Western civilization.

Since many of the original recipes of this period contain raw eggs, they have all been reformulated with cooked eggs. Unfortunately, this adds a tiny bit more work to these recipes. We apologize for any inconvenience, but your safety is our main concern.

So, look, it won't kill the cake if you don't use cream of tartar in your egg whites. It also won't kill you to pick some up on your next shopping trip. The results will be worth it.

Be a smarty-pants: Assemble all ingredients first. You will be a grade-A egghead and be ready to bake with flour power.

MEASURING

Hi, I'm Milton the Measuring Cup with some handy measuring tips for you . . . Measure correctly and your cakes and cookies will come out eggs-actly as planned.

Do You Know the Way to (Measure Ingredients in) San Jose?

A dry measuring cup is rimless and spoutless and has a flat top. It is designed to hold an exact amount when filled to its tippy top. Measure quarter cups in "quarter cup" measuring cups. Measure half cups in "halves," and so on. Lightly scoop flour, sugar, or other "dry" ingredients into your dry measuring cup. Do not tamp down, shake, or compress (the ingredients, that is). With the back of a knife, scrape the excess off the top. Never try to eyeball smaller amounts in bigger cups, even if they have markings on the sides. It's just not an accurate way of measuring.

For liquids, use clear "liquid" measuring cups. Place the cup on a level surface and pour the liquid up to the desired marking line. For accuracy, get down and read at eye level.

Lightly pack brown sugar into a dry measuring cup so that it just holds together. By the way, if your brown sugar turns rock hard, seal it up with a piece of cut apple or a lettuce leaf. It should recover from much of its geological status in twenty-four hours.

Amorphous globs, such as peanut butter or vegetable shortening, can be packed into dry measuring cups or measured with the water displacement method. Here is an example: To measure $1/4$ cup of peanut butter, fill a 2-cup liquid measure with 1 cup of water. Scoop in peanut butter until the water measures $1^1/4$ cups. Remove the peanut butter and lightly dry with a paper towel.

Use measuring spoons as if they were cups. Fill them to the top with liquids. Overfill them with dry ingredients, then scrape off the excess with the back of a knife.

A SPRITZ IN TIME

Whenever possible, use baking parchment and/or nonstick vegetable spray (like Pam). They keep cakes and cookies from sticking to pans and make cleanup as easy as pie.

*E*nter the cake mix and a new baking era. In a country that was eager for instant this and instant that, mixes gave the satisfaction of preparing something homemade, in a quarter of the time! Soon after the fifties began, companies like Pillsbury were mass-producing a variety of cake mixes. By 1957, the choices were enormous. Frostings, alone, were available in chocolate fudge, fluffy white, chocolate malt, peanut creme, and bright pink cherry fluff. But, flour, shortening, and other "scratch" ingredient manufacturers put up a valiant defense. Their main pitch was the "new" and "easy" recipe. Some of these cakes were downright silly but many were creative and far more original than the stuff available in mix form. The ante would soon rise. In 1957, Pillsbury introduced "Cake 'n' Frosting Mix—You get *Both* in *One* Package!" Three years later, following the success of their frozen cheesecakes, Sara Lee introduced prepacked banana and orange cakes. All you had to do was thaw.

Follow these simple steps for perfect cakes.

1. Organize all of your ingredients first. You want to function at the junction—not have a conniption in the kitchen.

2. Baking parchment is wonderful for lining cake pans. Cakes release easily and cleanup becomes a cinch. Just cut the parchment into rounds, rectangles, or whatever shape is appropriate and fit it into the bottoms of your pans.

3. Although any of these cakes can be prepared with ordinary electric hand mixers,

stationary mixers, like the ones made by Kitchenaid, are absolutely the best tools a baker can own, but sometimes ingredients stick to the sides or bottom. It is good policy to stop the engines and scrape the bowl down with a rubber spatula.

4. Ovens vary in temperature and may have hot spots. Halfway through baking, give the pans a turn—front to back. Be flexible and keep an eye on the cake. Timers don't say, "Done." They say, "Go and check."

5. Buy two of the exact same 9-inch cake pans. After baking, just trim the tops evenly and you will have two perfect layers. You may also bake a cake in one pan and slice it into layers. Just remember to allow more time for baking.

6. For a clean and even-looking cake, flip the top layer over, so its smooth bottom will be the top of the cake.

7. Many of the cakes in this book are interchangeable. Be adventurous and substitute, for example, yellow cake for buttermilk, hot milk sponge for cupcakes.

8. There are several tests for doneness: The center springs back when lightly pressed. A cake tester comes out clean, etc. Cakes that pull from the sides of the pan have reached their optimum expansion. Remove them from the oven or, if they are still liquid in the center, turn the oven down to finish.

"Daddy, do we always have to presift?"

How many times does your child ask that question? Do you know the real answer? If your cakes are dull, flat, and lifeless, perhaps you are not presifting the way you should. Follow these easy steps to ensure lighter, fluffier, moister cakes.

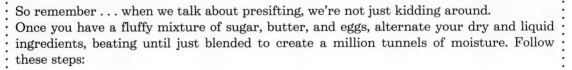

1. Measure out all ingredients.
2. Triple sifters are fine, but the easiest way to sift is by passing the ingredients through a large sieve. Catch the ingredients in a large bowl or on a large piece of paper.
3. Repeat two more times.

So remember . . . when we talk about presifting, we're not just kidding around. Once you have a fluffy mixture of sugar, butter, and eggs, alternate your dry and liquid ingredients, beating until just blended to create a million tunnels of moisture. Follow these steps:

1. Beat in a third of the flour mixture.
2. Beat in half of the liquids.
3. Beat in another third of the flour mixture.
4. Beat in the remaining half of the liquids.
5. Beat in the final third of the flour mixture.

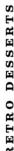

CRAZY CRATERS OF THE MOON CAKE WITH MOONROCK TOPPING

Break every rule of baking and still come up with a phenomenal, and low-fat, cake. The scrumptious madness of Crazy Cake is in the method. It's an out-of-this-world treat, both to make and eat, for chocoholic lunar-tics of every age.

✦✦✦✦✦✦✦✦✦✦✦✦✦✦✦✦✦✦✦✦✦✦✦✦✦✦✦✦✦✦

1½ cups all-purpose flour
1¼ cups sugar
¼ cup unsweetened Dutch-processed cocoa
1 teaspoon baking soda
¼ teaspoon salt
6 tablespoons vegetable oil (or try melted unsalted butter)

1 tablespoon cider or white vinegar
1 teaspoon vanilla extract
1 cup milk
½ cup miniature marshmallows, or ½-inch pieces of marshmallow (see page 184 for homemade)

✦✦✦✦✦✦✦✦✦✦✦✦✦✦✦✦✦✦✦✦✦✦✦✦✦✦✦✦✦✦

1. Set a rack in the middle of the oven and preheat to 350°F.

2. In an 8-inch round cake pan, mix together the flour, sugar, cocoa, baking soda, and salt.

3. With a spoon, dig one 1½-inch and two ¾-inch holes (or craters) in the flour mixture. Put the oil in the big hole and vinegar and vanilla in the small holes. (Yes, the vinegar does start to bubble up like a volcano.)

4. Pour the milk over everything and mix to the consistency of mud.

5. Bake for 15 minutes, then sprinkle on the marshmallows. Continue baking for 10 to 15 additional minutes, or until the center springs back when lightly pressed and the marshmallows melt into tanned "moon rocks." Set the pan on a rack to cool. Serve this right out of the pan.

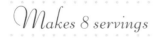
Makes 8 servings

CHOCOLATE BLACKOUT CAKE

In kinder, gentler times, there were no reported deaths by chocolate. This chocolate cake—Devil's Food filled with chocolate pudding and frosted with crunchy cake crumbs—could, allegedly, deliver a blast so chocolatey-good that the taster might be knocked into unconsciousness, but it was too good a cake to commit manslaughter.

Blackout cakes were rarely made at home. They were the products of bakeries, like the famous Ebinger's, where there was always a ready supply of cake crumbs. Some, like ours, were frosted. Others had just an outer schmear of pudding to hold the crumbs on.

✦✦✦✦✦✦✦✦✦✦✦✦✦✦✦✦✦✦✦✦✦✦✦✦✦✦✦✦✦✦

FOR THE DEVIL'S FOOD CAKE
Nonstick vegetable spray for coating the
    pan
1¼ cups cake flour
½ cup unsweetened Dutch-process cocoa
1 teaspoon baking soda
¼ teaspoon baking powder
½ teaspoon salt
10 tablespoons (1¼ sticks) unsalted butter
    at room temperature
1½ cups sugar
3 large eggs
½ cup buttermilk
1 teaspoon vanilla extract
½ cup brewed strong coffee

FOR THE GANACHE FROSTING
4 ounces semisweet chocolate, coarsely
    chopped
½ cup heavy cream
½ recipe Chocolate Pudding (page 96)

✦✦✦✦✦✦✦✦✦✦✦✦✦✦✦✦✦✦✦✦✦✦✦✦✦✦✦✦

1. Make the Devil's Food Cake: Set a rack in the middle of the oven and preheat to 350°F. Lightly coat an 8-inch cake pan with nonstick vegetable spray and line the bottom with a circle of baking parchment.

2. Into a large bowl, sift the flour, cocoa, baking soda, baking powder, and salt together—three times.

3. In a mixing bowl, beat the butter and sugar together at high speed for 15 seconds, until combined. Add the eggs, one at a time, beating until each is incorporated. Continue beating until light and fluffy, about 6 minutes more.

4. With the mixer on its lowest setting, beat in one-third of the flour mixture. Beat in the buttermilk and vanilla, then another third of the flour mixture. Beat in the coffee and then the remaining flour.

5. Spread the batter in the prepared pan and bake for 30 to 40 minutes, or until the center springs back when lightly pressed and a cake tester comes out clean. Set the pan on a rack to cool. Leave the oven on.

6. Make the Ganache Frosting: Put the chocolate in a small bowl. Over medium heat, bring the cream just to the simmering point. Pour the hot cream over the chocolate. Working from the center out, gently stir with a whisk to melt and blend. Continue stirring until smooth. Let sit for 30 minutes to thicken until spreadable.

7. To assemble: Turn the cake out of the pan and trim the top with a large serrated knife so the top is flat. Reserve the scraps. Slice the cake horizontally into 3 layers. In a 350°F oven, toast the scraps on a baking sheet for 5 minutes. Let cool, then coarsely chop in a food processor. Don't make them too fine. An uneven texture is ideal.

8. Spread the chocolate pudding between the layers. Frost the cake with the ganache, then coat the sides with the crunchy crumbs.

Makes one 8-inch cake or 8 servings

Red Velvet Cake

It was believed that a devil's food cake would have even more sinfully good attributes if it somehow took on a red hue. The simple solution was to add a solution of red food coloring—often a whole bottle of it—and . . . *voilà*, the emperor's new clothes. Go figure.

Standing tall was always the pride of a blackout cake; this is why we bake it in an 8-inch pan. You may make this cake in a 9-inch pan. Reduce the baking time by 5 minutes.

FLUFFY-FROSTED COCONUT LAYER CAKE,
DINER-STYLE STRAWBERRY SHORTCAKE, AND
CHOCOLATE BLACKOUT CAKE

FLUFFY-FROSTED COCONUT LAYER CAKE

. . . .

The fluffy cakes in the Pillsbury ads used coconut straight out of the bag, but light toasting will add a whole lot of flavor and texture. Check out the instructions on page 3. We also prefer unsweetened flakes or chips, which are available in health food stores and Asian markets.

Down South they liked to use white cake. Up North yellow cake was the cake of choice. Down South they also like Divinity icing; White Mountain is just a bit more workable.

◆◆◆◆◆◆◆◆◆◆◆◆◆◆◆◆◆◆◆◆◆◆◆◆◆◆◆◆

FOR THE YELLOW CAKE
Nonstick vegetable spray for coating
   the pan
2¼ cups cake flour
2½ teaspoons baking powder
½ teaspoon salt
½ cup (1 stick) unsalted butter at room
   temperature
1¼ cups sugar
2 large eggs
¾ cups milk
2 teaspoons vanilla extract
1 teaspoon framboise, almond extract,
   or orange extract

FOR THE WHITE MOUNTAIN FROSTING
½ cup water
1½ cups sugar
3 large egg whites
¼ teaspoon cream of tartar
Pinch of salt
2 teaspoons vanilla extract
1½ cups unsweetened coconut flakes,
   lightly toasted (page 3)

◆◆◆◆◆◆◆◆◆◆◆◆◆◆◆◆◆◆◆◆◆◆◆◆◆◆◆

1. Make the Yellow Cake: Set a rack in the middle of the oven and preheat to 350°F. Lightly coat two 9-inch cake pans with nonstick vegetable spray. Line the bottoms with a circle of baking parchment.

2. Into a large bowl, sift the flour, baking powder, and salt together—three times.

3. In a mixing bowl, beat the butter and sugar together at high speed for 15 seconds, until combined. Add the eggs, one at a time, beating until each is incorporated. Continue beating until light and fluffy, about 6 minutes more.

4. With the mixer on its lowest setting, beat in one-third of the flour mixture. Beat in half of the milk and all of the vanilla and framboise, then another third of the flour mixture. Beat in the remaining milk and then the remaining flour.

5. Spread the batter in the prepared pans and bake for 20 minutes, or until golden brown, the center springs back when lightly pressed, and a cake tester comes out clean. Set the pans on a rack to cool. Turn the cakes out of the pans and trim the tops with a large serrated knife so the tops are flat. Slice each cake horizontally into 2 layers.

6. While the cakes are baking, make the White Mountain Frosting: Combine the water and sugar in a small saucepan fitted with a candy thermometer. Over high heat, bring the temperature to 240°F (soft ball). In the meantime, in a completely clean, dry bowl, whisk the egg whites, cream of tartar, salt, and vanilla until creamy, foamy, and barely able to hold very soft peaks. While whisking slowly, carefully drizzle in the hot syrup. Continue to whisk on high speed until fluffy, firm, and just warm.

7. Divide the frosting into 2 batches. Fold ½ cup of the coconut into half of the frosting. Spread a ¼-inch layer of this coconut frosting between each cake layer. Frost the outside of the cake with the remaining frosting and then coat the cake with the remaining toasted coconut.

Makes one 9-inch cake or 12 servings

So, what do you do if there's no thermometer in the house? You can make a very legitimate alternative to White Mountain Frosting called 7-Minute, or Boiled, Frosting.

1½ cups sugar
¼ teaspoon cream of tartar
Pinch of salt
4 large egg whites
¼ cup water
2 teaspoons vanilla extract

Combine all of the ingredients except the vanilla in a large, clean bowl and set over a pan of simmering water. Whisk constantly until the mixture is the temperature of very hot bathwater—160°F. (If you dipped your toe in, you would have to rethink the situation. You know what I'm sayin'?) Remove from the heat and continue to whisk (you can switch to an electric mixer) until the frosting has the consistency of shaving cream. Whisk in the vanilla.

DINER-STYLE STRAWBERRY SHORTCAKE

O.K. So it's luscious, it's scrumptious, it's big and beautiful, but it's not really a short-cake.

Diners have always passed off what should be called a strawberry sponge cake as the real McCoy. But then again, it often wasn't even a real sponge cake, but a "hot-milk sponge cake," which is more like a butter cake . . . Oh a rose is a rose is a cake.

Some like to coat the pan with an additional layer of flour. This just adds an unpleasant layer of paste to the cake. This cake has a tendency to stick to the pan. If that turns out to be the case, run a knife around the edge to loosen it.

❖❖❖❖❖❖❖❖❖❖❖❖❖❖❖❖❖❖❖❖❖❖❖❖❖

Nonstick vegetable spray for coating the pans

FOR THE HOT-MILK SPONGE CAKE
1½ cups cake flour
1½ teaspoons baking powder
½ teaspoon salt
¾ cup milk
3 tablespoons unsalted butter
1 tablespoon vanilla extract
1 teaspoon lemon extract
3 large eggs
1¼ cups sugar
2 pints fresh strawberries

FOR THE WHIPPED CREAM FROSTING
1 teaspoon gelatin
2 cups heavy cream
½ cup confectioners' sugar
2 teaspoons vanilla extract

❖❖❖❖❖❖❖❖❖❖❖❖❖❖❖❖❖❖❖❖❖❖❖❖

1. Set a rack in the middle of the oven and preheat to 350°F. Lightly coat two 9-inch cake pans with nonstick vegetable spray. Line the bottoms with a circle of baking parchment.

2. Make the Hot-Milk Sponge Cake: Into a large bowl, sift the flour, baking powder, and salt together—three times.

3. In a small saucepan, bring the milk and butter to a boil. Remove from the heat and add the vanilla and lemon extracts.

4. In a mixing bowl, beat the eggs and sugar until pale yellow, fluffy, and doubled in volume. While still beating, drizzle in the hot milk mixture. Fold in the flour mixture.

5. Spread the batter in the prepared pans and bake for 15 minutes, or until golden, the center springs back when lightly pressed, and a cake tester comes out clean. Set the pans on a rack to cool.

6. Run the tip of a knife around the edges of the cakes to loosen them, and turn them out of the pans.

7. Wash and dry the strawberries. Pick out the 12 best. Stem and slice the rest.

8. Make the Whipped Cream Frosting: In a medium bowl, mix together the gelatin and ¼ cup of the cream. Let rest for 5 minutes to soften, then place the bowl over barely simmering water until the gelatin has completely dissolved. Remove the bowl from the heat and let cool to tepid. In the meantime, in a mixing bowl, whip the rest of the cream until slightly thickened. Add the confectioners' sugar and vanilla and whip to the consistency of shaving cream. Fold ½ cup of the whipped cream into the gelatin mixture, then fold in the rest.

9. To assemble: Lay the sliced berries over 1 cake, then spread a ½-inch layer of whipped cream on top. Place the second cake over the first. Frost the entire cake with the remaining whipped cream. Top with the 12 whole berries.

Makes one 9-inch cake or 12 servings

For a professional look, run the thickest tines of a cake comb around the circumference of the cake to put a striped pattern in the whipped cream.

BOSTON CREAM PIE

This is, in reality, a cake, but it is baked in a pie plate, hence the name.

❖❖❖❖❖❖❖❖❖❖❖❖❖❖❖❖❖❖❖❖❖❖❖❖❖❖❖❖❖

Nonstick vegetable spray for coating the pan

1 recipe batter for Hot-Milk Sponge Cake (see Diner-Style Strawberry Shortcake, page 14, steps 2–4)

1 recipe Pastry Cream (see Vanilla Pudding, page 100)

1 recipe Chocolate Glaze (page 46)

❖❖❖❖❖❖❖❖❖❖❖❖❖❖❖❖❖❖❖❖❖❖❖❖❖❖❖❖❖

1. Set a rack in the middle of the oven and preheat to 350°F. Lightly coat a 9-inch pie pan with nonstick vegetable spray.

2. Prepare the batter for the Hot-Milk Sponge Cake as directed. Pour the batter into the prepared pan and bake for 20 minutes, until golden brown, the center springs back when lightly pressed, and a cake tester comes out clean. Set the pan on a rack to cool.

3. With a long serrated knife, cut off the domed top half of the pie. Spread the Pastry Cream on the bottom half and replace the top. Pour on the glaze and, with as few strokes as possible, spread with a metal spatula.

Makes one 9-inch pie . . . uh, cake or 8 servings

In 1956, Pillsbury featured some clever things to do with their thirteen-egg angel food cake mix. In an ad, the cakes were "all dolled up for summer," shortcake style for "Strawberried up," and à la mode with fudge sauce for "Chocolate all the way."

LIME-RICKEY ANGEL FOOD CAKE

Once upon a time there was a candy store on every city street corner and a soda shop in every town. Soda jerks could get very creative, inventing concoctions like the Chocolate Egg Cream and the Cherry Coke. This angel food cake takes its inspiration from the Lime Rickey, a seltzer solution of lime with raspberry or cherry syrups. It's a very berry "un-cola."

❖❖❖❖❖❖❖❖❖❖❖❖❖❖❖❖❖❖❖❖❖❖❖❖❖❖

1¼ cups cake flour
¾ teaspoon baking powder
¼ cup confectioners' sugar
1 cup egg whites (7 to 8 large eggs)
¼ teaspoon salt

Pinch of cream of tartar
½ cup granulated sugar
Grated zest and juice of 1 lime
½ cup Melba Sauce (page 124)

❖❖❖❖❖❖❖❖❖❖❖❖❖❖❖❖❖❖❖❖❖❖❖❖❖❖

1. Set a rack in the middle of the oven and preheat to 325°F.

2. Into a large bowl, sift the flour, baking powder, and confectioners' sugar—three times.

3. In a completely clean, dry mixing bowl, on high speed, whisk the egg whites, salt, and cream of tartar until creamy and foamy and barely able to hold soft peaks. With the mixer still running, sprinkle in the granulated sugar. Continue to whisk on high speed until the egg whites hold very soft peaks that are the consistency of shaving cream. Whisk in the lime zest and juice.

4. In thirds, sprinkle the flour mixture over the egg whites and gently fold in. Spread the batter in an ungreased 10-inch angel food pan (a tube pan with a removable bottom). Level the batter with a metal spatula and bake for 25 to 30 minutes, until lightly tanned and the center springs back when lightly pressed. To cool, invert the tube pan, upside down, over a bottle.

5. To remove the cake, run a knife around the edge of the pan to loosen it. Invert onto a plate and remove the bottom and pan. Invert again, right side up, onto a serving platter. Drizzle on the Melba Sauce in a swirly or crisscross pattern.

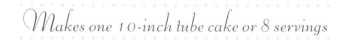

Makes one 10-inch tube cake or 8 servings

PEANUT BUTTER–BANANA
SANDWICH CAKE

Make dessert time fun time by turning a classic combo into a sensation. Along with "Cake Split" and "Nutty Pie Cake," the "Inside-Out" cake sandwich was introduced as part of Betty Crocker's 1957 "Crazy mixed-up cakes" ad campaign. The next year, fudge frosting between two slices of white cake was called a "Lunch-box trick! A wholesome noontime treat!"

Try carving this delicious banana cake into sandwiches . . . filled with peanut butter buttercream and sliced bananas!

◆◆◆◆◆◆◆◆◆◆◆◆◆◆◆◆◆◆◆◆◆◆◆◆◆◆◆◆◆

FOR THE BANANA CAKE
Nonstick vegetable spray for coating the pan
2½ cups cake flour
1 teaspoon baking soda
¼ teaspoon baking powder
¼ teaspoon salt
¾ cup (1½ sticks) unsalted butter at room temperature
1¼ cups sugar
3 large eggs
3 large, ripe bananas
½ cup sour cream
1 teaspoon vanilla extract

FOR THE PEANUT BUTTER BUTTERCREAM
½ cup (1 stick) unsalted butter at room temperature
1 cup creamy peanut butter
1¼ cups sifted confectioners' sugar

TO ASSEMBLE
4 bananas
Ice cream
Chocolate Fudge Sauce (page 199)

◆◆◆◆◆◆◆◆◆◆◆◆◆◆◆◆◆◆◆◆◆◆◆◆◆◆◆◆◆

1. Make the Banana Cake: Set a rack in the middle of the oven and preheat to 350°F. Lightly coat a 6-cup loaf pan with nonstick vegetable spray. Line the bottom with a rectangle of baking parchment.

2. Into a large bowl, sift the flour, baking soda, baking powder, and salt together—three times.

3. In a mixing bowl, beat the butter and sugar together at high speed for 15 seconds, until combined. Add the eggs, one at a time, beating until each is incorporated. Continue beating until light and fluffy, about 6 minutes more.

4. In a medium bowl, mash the bananas until soupy. Stir in the sour cream and vanilla.

5. With the mixer on its lowest setting, beat in one-third of the flour mixture. Beat in half of

the banana mixture, then another third of the flour. Beat in the remaining banana mixture and then the remaining flour.

6. Spread the batter in the prepared pan and bake for 40 minutes, or until the center springs back when lightly pressed and a cake tester comes out clean. Set the pan on a rack to cool.

7. Make the Peanut Butter Buttercream: On medium speed, beat the butter and peanut butter in a mixing bowl until blended. Reduce the speed to low and gradually beat in the confectioners' sugar. Increase the speed to high and beat for 3 to 5 minutes, until smooth and fluffy.

8. Turn the cooled cake out of the pan. With a serrated knife, trim off the end crusts and cut the loaf into ½-inch slices. Peel the bananas and cut them into ¼-inch-thick rounds. Spread half the cake slices with the buttercream and layer on the banana slices. Place the remaining cake slices on top to form sandwiches. Cut the sandwiches in half and serve with ice cream and Chocolate Fudge Sauce.

Makes 8 sandwiches

If a sandwich could win *"Miss Congeniality,"* it would have to be peanut butter and jelly. But it wasn't always the fairest in the land. Peanut butter was first invented as a dietary supplement for the toothless. Elvis's favorite sandwich, peanut butter and bacon, was so popular that Oscar Mayer actually produced the combo in a loaf. However, soon after its introduction, it was PB&J that became the overwhelming people's choice.

Always bake with ripe or very ripe bananas. The skins should be speckled with black and show no signs of green. The flesh should be soft but not stringy or watery.

As Louis Prima recommended in the song of the same name, "Please no squeeza da banana." When you do that (much to the chagrin of your greengrocer), "you make the banana flat."

RASPBERRY-COCONUT
JELLY ROLL

M̶oist sponge cake is filled with raspberry preserves, rolled around cream filling, and coated in toasted coconut. It's fun. It's easy. And it's sure to make everyone happy because it's sticky and gooey and juicy and gr-r-r-eat!

✦✦✦✦✦✦✦✦✦✦✦✦✦✦✦✦✦✦✦✦✦✦✦✦✦✦✦✦✦

Nonstick vegetable spray for coating
   parchment
½ cup cake flour
⅛ teaspoon baking powder
4 large eggs, separated
1 teaspoon vanilla extract
½ cup sugar, divided
Pinch of salt
Pinch of cream of tartar
½ teaspoon confectioners' sugar

Vanilla Cream Filling (page 36)
½ cup raspberry preserves or jam
2 tablespoons water
1¼ cups toasted (page 3) unsweetened
   coconut flakes

✦✦✦✦✦✦✦✦✦✦✦✦✦✦✦✦✦✦✦✦✦✦✦✦✦✦✦✦✦

1. Set a rack in the middle of the oven and preheat to 350°F. Line a 10½- by 15½-inch jelly roll pan with baking parchment and lightly coat with nonstick vegetable spray.

2. Into a large bowl, sift the flour and baking powder together—three times.

3. In a mixing bowl, beat the egg yolks, vanilla, and ¼ cup of the sugar together until thick, pale yellow, and, get this, when drizzled from the beater, it will hold a ribbon shape for 2 seconds on the surface. This should take about 5 minutes.

4. Fold in the flour mixture.

5. In another clean, dry mixing bowl, whisk the egg whites with the pinches of salt and cream of tartar until creamy and foamy. With the mixer still running, sprinkle in the remaining ¼ cup sugar and whisk until the egg whites hold very soft peaks—the consistency of shaving cream.

6. In thirds, fold the egg whites into the egg yolk mixture. Spread the batter in the prepared pan and bake for 8 minutes, until barely golden. Set the pan on a rack to cool.

7. Run the tip of a knife around the edge of the cake to loosen it from the sides. Dust the surface with the confectioners' sugar. Flip the cake onto a dry work surface. With an

offset spatula, spread a ⅛-inch-thick layer of vanilla cream over the cake. Mix the preserves and water until smooth, then carefully spread one-third of it in a very thin layer over the vanilla cream. Roll up tightly. Spread the rest of the preserves around the outside of the roll. Sprinkle the coconut on a cookie sheet. Roll the cake through the coconut to coat completely. Refrigerate for 1 hour to set, then trim the ends even.

Makes one 10½-inch jelly roll or 8 servings

What about fresh coconut?

If you had a hammer, you could hammer that coconut in the morning. You could also bake it. Then pry the shell off. Then skin off the pellicle. Then shred it . . . all da-a-a-y. Trust me, fresh coconut ends up tasting about the same as the dried stuff.

RUM & CHERRY COLA MARBLE CAKE

Cola, as it turns out, is a darn good flavor for cake and a nifty complement for chocolate. Unfortunately, many cola cakes were fluffy, saccharin-tasting ordeals. This is a compilation of several old-school rum cakes, in a rum & Coca-Cola tribute to the Andrews Sisters. And speaking of the Andrews Sisters . . . In reverence to Patti, La Verne, and Maxene, Coke would probably be the politically correct cola to use, but Pepsi, RC, or even that prune-flavored favorite, Dr Pepper, will all work.

✦✦✦✦✦✦✦✦✦✦✦✦✦✦✦✦✦✦✦✦✦✦✦✦✦✦✦

FOR THE CHERRY COLA MARBLE CAKE
½ cup cola
½ cup dried sour cherries
3 ounces semisweet chocolate
1 ounce unsweetened chocolate
Nonstick vegetable spray for coating
    the pan
2 cups all-purpose flour
2 teaspoons baking powder
¼ teaspoon salt
¾ cup (1½ sticks) unsalted butter at room
    temperature
1¼ cups sugar
4 large eggs

FOR THE RUM & COLA SYRUP
1 cup cola
¼ cup dark rum
¼ cup sugar

✦✦✦✦✦✦✦✦✦✦✦✦✦✦✦✦✦✦✦✦✦✦✦✦

1. In a small saucepan, bring the cola and dried cherries to a boil. Remove from the heat and set aside for 30 minutes.

2. Melt the chocolates in a completely dry bowl or double boiler set over barely simmering water. Set aside in a warm place until ready to use.

3. Set a rack in the middle of the oven and preheat to 375°F. Lightly coat a 6-cup loaf pan or Bundt pan with nonstick vegetable spray and line the bottom with a rectangle of baking parchment.

4. Into a large bowl, sift the flour, baking powder, and salt together—three times.

5. In a mixing bowl, beat the butter and sugar together at high speed for 15 seconds, until combined. Add the eggs, one at a time, beating until each is incorporated. Continue beating until light and fluffy, about 6 more minutes.

6. With the mixer on its lowest setting, gradually beat in the flour mixture.

7. Fold the cherries and their liquid into half of the batter and spread it in the bottom of the pan. Fold the melted chocolate into the remaining batter and add it to the pan. Bake for 30 minutes, or until springy, completely set, and a cake tester comes out clean. Set the pan on a rack to cool.

8. Make the Rum & Cola Syrup: In a small saucepan, boil the cola, rum, and sugar until all of the crystals are dissolved. Remove the cake from the pan by inverting onto a serving platter and soak with the syrup.

Makes 8 servings

In 1949, Charles Lubin developed an aluminum pan that he could bake, freeze, and market his cheesecakes in. He named the thawable cakes after his daughter, Sara Lee. Today the company is a multimillion-dollar conglomerate that makes dozens of different baked goods and several lines of pantyhose.

EGGNOG CHEESECAKE

Philadelphia brand cream cheese once promoted their product by giving out recipes for "Hollywood Cheesecake." Cheesecakes in Hollywood were not just the figments of some ad exec's imagination.

On I Dream of Jeannie, *Barbara Eden couldn't make a cookie without crossing her arms and wishing for it, but in real life she was quite an accomplished baker. Her husband, Michael Ansara (he played Cochise on the TV western* Broken Arrow)*, bragged about her luscious "New York" cheesecake. As for eggnog, rumor has it that Robert Mitchum's has always been the best in Hollywood.*

Before you start, set your cream cheese and butter out for several hours, so it can warm up to room temperature.

❖❖❖❖❖❖❖❖❖❖❖❖❖❖❖❖❖❖❖❖❖❖❖❖

FOR THE WALNUT-GRAHAM CRUST
6 tablespoons (¾ stick) unsalted butter, melted, plus 1 tablespoon for coating the pan
1 cup graham cracker crumbs
2 tablespoons sugar
½ cup chopped walnuts, lightly toasted (page 3)

FOR THE CAKE BATTER
1½ pounds cream cheese at room temperature
6 tablespoons (¾ stick) unsalted butter at room temperature
1 cup sugar
3 tablespoons cornstarch
1 tablespoon ground nutmeg
4 large eggs
1 cup sour cream
¼ cup plus 2 tablespoons cream sherry, such as Dry Sack or Harvey's

❖❖❖❖❖❖❖❖❖❖❖❖❖❖❖❖❖❖❖❖❖❖❖❖

1. Make the Walnut-Graham Crust: Coat an 8-inch cake pan or foil-wrapped 8-inch spring-form with 1 tablespoon of the melted butter.

2. Combine the graham cracker crumbs, sugar, and walnuts in a medium bowl. Add the 6 tablespoons of melted butter and mix thoroughly. Pat the mixture evenly over the bottom of the prepared cake pan.

3. Set a rack in the bottom third of the oven and preheat to 300°F.

4. Make the Cake Batter: Combine the cream cheese, butter, sugar, cornstarch, and nutmeg in a large mixing bowl and beat at medium speed just until blended. Take care not to mix too much air into the batter. Add the eggs, one at a time, until each is incorporated. Reduce the speed and beat in the sour cream and sherry.

5. Pour the batter into the prepared cake pan. Set the cake pan in a roasting pan and pour about 1 inch of hot water into the larger pan. Cover the roasting pan with foil and bake for 1 hour. Remove the foil and bake for 15 to 30 more minutes, until lightly tanned, slightly puffed, and barely firm. Cool to room temperature right in the water bath. Remove from the bath and refrigerate overnight.

6. To release the cake from a 1-piece pan: Pop it into a 350°F oven for 2 minutes, then invert it onto a plate covered with plastic wrap or foil. Give it a shake. *Voilà!* Now turn it right side up onto a serving platter and peel off the foil or plastic. For a springform, pop the cake into the oven for 2 minutes and un-spring. This cake will last for 4 days, covered, in the refrigerator.

Makes an 8-inch cake or 8 servings

DESSERTS *on the* DIAL: *I Dream of Jeannie*

Out of jealousy, Jeannie once spiked a cake with a potion that made Tony and Dr. Bellows act like little kids. Incidentally, chocolate fans, the action for *I Dream of Jeannie* took place in Cocoa Beach.

On *Green Acres,* Lisa actually attempted to bake a cake!

JACK-O'-LANTERN CHEESECAKES

For a spooky Halloween treat, hollow out mini or munchkin pumpkins and fill them with a spiced cheesecake batter. Slowly bake and chill, then serve with glowing birthday candles. Little ghosts and goblins will haunt your house, looking for more.

Before you start, set your cream cheese and butter out for several hours, so they can warm up to room temperature.

Eight ½-pound mini pumpkins
1½ pounds cream cheese at room temperature
6 tablespoons (¾ stick) unsalted butter at room temperature
1 cup lightly packed light brown sugar
6 tablespoons granulated sugar
2 tablespoons plus 1 teaspoon cornstarch
1 tablespoon ground cinnamon
2 teaspoons ground ginger
¾ teaspoon ground cloves
4 large eggs
1 cup sour cream
1 teaspoon vanilla extract
1 cup pumpkin puree (canned is just fine)

FOR THE CRANBERRY TOPPING
¾ cup orange juice
½ cup sugar
1 teaspoon vanilla extract
½ pound fresh or frozen cranberries

Birthday candles and mint leaves for garnish (optional)

1. Set a rack in the middle of the oven and preheat to 300°F.

2. Cut the tops off the pumpkins and set aside. With a teaspoon or grapefruit knife, scrape the fibrous pulp and seeds out of each pumpkin. Scrape some of the meat off the inner walls so they are no more than ⅜ inch thick, discarding the pumpkin meat.

3. Combine the cream cheese, butter, sugars, cornstarch, cinnamon, ginger, and cloves in a large mixing bowl and beat at medium speed until blended. Take care not to mix too much air into the batter. Add the eggs, one at a time, beating until each is incorporated. Reduce the speed and beat in the sour cream, vanilla, and pumpkin puree.

4. Fill the pumpkin shells with the batter and bake on a cookie sheet for 15 minutes. Turn the pan and place the tops next to the pumpkins. Bake for 10 more minutes, until barely set and firm. If at any time the cakes start to puff up, turn the temperature down or remove them. Let cool in the pan on a rack, then refrigerate.

5. Make the Cranberry Topping: Combine all the ingredients in a medium saucepan, heat to a boil, then reduce the heat and simmer for 10 minutes, until the berries have popped and form a thick sauce. Let cool.

6. To serve, spoon cranberry topping over the filling. Place the pumpkin lid on at a jaunty angle. Stick the birthday candle and mint sprig into the top.

Makes 8 individual cheesecakes

CHECKERBOARD CAKE

Oh, what an amazing feat of engineering. You pipe out circles and they end up checkers. Cooking equipment stores sell checkerboard cake sets with nifty little dividers to help you spread the batter in even rings. They are absolutely the way to go and well worth the investment. For the Grizzly Adams types among us, we have also included instructions for winging it with a pencil and a compass.

✦✦✦✦✦✦✦✦✦✦✦✦✦✦✦✦✦✦✦✦✦✦✦✦✦✦✦✦✦

FOR THE CAKE
Nonstick vegetable spray for coating pans
2¾ cups cake flour
1 tablespoon baking powder
½ teaspoon salt
¾ cup (1½ sticks) unsalted butter at room
     temperature
1¾ cups sugar, divided
6 large eggs, separated
1 teaspoon vanilla extract
2 tablespoons orange liqueur, Frangelico,
     or Amaretto
1 cup milk
Pinch of salt
Pinch of cream of tartar
3 tablespoons unsweetened Dutch-
     processed cocoa

FOR THE EVAPORATED-MILK FROSTING
8 ounces semisweet chocolate
¾ cup evaporated milk
¼ cup unsalted butter at room
     temperature

✦✦✦✦✦✦✦✦✦✦✦✦✦✦✦✦✦✦✦✦✦✦✦✦✦✦✦✦

1. Make the Cake: Set a rack in the middle of the oven and preheat to 350°F. Cut three 9-inch parchment circles. Measuring from the outer edges, draw two 1½-inch-wide concentric circles on each. This will leave a 3-inch circle in the center. Coat three 9-inch cake pans with nonstick vegetable spray and line their bottoms with the parchment circles, ink side down.

2. Into a large bowl, sift the flour, baking powder, and salt together—three times.

3. In a mixing bowl, beat together the butter and 1¼ cups of the sugar at high speed until combined. Add the egg yolks, two at a time, beating until incorporated. Continue beating until pale yellow and thickened, about 3 minutes more.

4. Using the slowest setting, beat one-third of the flour mixture into the wet mixture. Beat in the vanilla, liqueur, and half of the milk, then beat in another third of the flour mixture. Beat in the rest of the milk and then the remaining flour mixture.

5. In a completely clean, dry bowl, whisk the egg whites, salt, and cream of tartar until very foamy. Still whisking, drizzle in the remaining ½ cup of sugar and whisk (on high speed) until the consistency of shaving cream.

6. Gently fold one-third of the egg whites into the batter. Fold in the remainder of the egg whites. Transfer two-thirds of the batter to a pastry bag fitted with a wide tube. Sift the cocoa on top of the remaining third and gently fold in. Transfer it to another pastry bag.

7. Pipe the white batter around the outer bands and center circles of two of the pans. Pipe the remaining white batter around the middle band of the third pan. Pipe chocolate batter into the remaining bands (2 inner bands, 1 outer band, and center). Bake the layers for 25 minutes, or until the centers spring back when lightly pressed. Set the pans on a rack to cool.

8. For the Evaporated-Milk Frosting: Finely chop the chocolate and place in a medium bowl. In a small saucepan, bring the evaporated milk just to the simmering point. Pour over the chocolate and gently stir with a whisk until smooth and blended. Let sit for 30 minutes to thicken. Beat in the butter.

9. Turn the cakes out of the pans. With a serrated knife, trim the cake layers so the tops are flat. Coat the top of a predominantly white layer with a thin layer of frosting. Stack the predominantly chocolate layer on top. Thinly frost the top of this second layer. Stack the last layer on, bottom side up. Frost the entire cake with the rest of the frosting.

Makes one 9-inch cake or 8 servings

CHOCOLATE PUDDING CAKE

More puddings than cakes, these dessert hybrids share a simple little trick: They make their own sauce. Like Patty Duke, they are identical cousins in some ways and worlds apart in others. The methods for making them are quite different, but when you get down to the basics, they are essentially mixed, baked, and . . . POOF: They magically separate into layers of cake and pudding. They can be made in a 9- by 9-inch square or 10-inch round cake pan, but since you'll want to spoon them right out of the pan that they're baked in, a lovely casserole would be best.

❖❖❖❖❖❖❖❖❖❖❖❖❖❖❖❖❖❖❖❖❖❖❖❖❖❖

Nonstick vegetable spray for coating dish
1 cup all-purpose flour
½ cup unsweetened Dutch-process cocoa, divided
2 teaspoons baking powder
¼ teaspoon salt
¾ cup granulated sugar
¾ cup chopped nuts (walnuts, pecans, or even hazelnuts will do)

¾ cup milk
1 teaspoon vanilla extract
2 tablespoons unsalted butter, melted
1 cup lightly packed light brown sugar
1¾ cups hot water
1 teaspoon vanilla extract

❖❖❖❖❖❖❖❖❖❖❖❖❖❖❖❖❖❖❖❖❖❖❖❖❖

1. Set a rack in the middle of the oven and preheat to 350°F. Lightly coat a 2-quart baking dish with nonstick vegetable spray.

2. Into a large bowl, sift the flour, ¼ cup of the cocoa, baking powder, salt, and granulated sugar. Stir in the nuts, milk, vanilla, and melted butter. Spread the batter in the prepared pan.

3. In a small bowl, mix together the brown sugar and remaining ¼ cup of cocoa. Sprinkle it on top of the batter. In another small bowl, mix the hot water and vanilla, and pour it over the cocoa. Bake for 30 minutes, until the top layer is set and just starts to pull from the sides. Serve warm, straight from the baking dish.

Makes 8 servings

LEMON PUDDING CAKE

Unlike its rich and dense chocolate relative, this Lemon Pudding Cake is delicate, tart, and light as a soufflé.

❖❖❖❖❖❖❖❖❖❖❖❖❖❖❖❖❖❖❖❖❖❖❖❖❖

Nonstick vegetable spray for coating dish
¼ cup all-purpose flour
¾ cup sugar, divided
1 cup milk
3 large eggs, separated
Grated zest of 2 lemons

¼ cup fresh lemon juice
½ teaspoon vanilla extract
¼ cup (½ stick) unsalted butter, melted
Pinch of salt

❖❖❖❖❖❖❖❖❖❖❖❖❖❖❖❖❖❖❖❖❖❖❖❖❖

1. Set a rack in the middle of the oven and preheat to 325°F. Lightly coat a 2-quart baking dish with nonstick vegetable spray.

2. Into a large bowl, sift the flour and ½ cup of the sugar together.

3. In a medium bowl, mix together the milk and egg yolks. Mix in the lemon zest, lemon juice, vanilla, and butter. Mix in the flour-sugar mixture

4. In the meantime, in a completely clean, dry bowl, on high speed, whisk the egg whites and salt until creamy and foamy. With the mixer still running, sprinkle in the remaining ¼ cup of sugar. Continue to whisk on high speed until the egg whites hold soft peaks that are the consistency of shaving cream.

5. Fold a quarter of the egg whites into the milk and yolk mixture. Fold in the rest of the whites. Pour the batter into the baking dish and set it in a roasting pan. Add enough hot water to come halfway up the sides of the baking dish. Bake for 30 minutes, until the top layer is set and light golden. Serve warm, straight from the baking dish.

Makes 8 servings

If I Knew You Were Comin', I'd Have Baked a Dozen Cupcakes

At some point, every baker is faced with the great decision: to be a big cake in a small bakery or to be a little cupcake in a big bakery. Cakes are luscious and gorgeous but cupcakes are adorable and fun. Why choose? The correct answer is to do both.

✦ *Flashback*

Every Sunday, young Elvis and his father would get up early and take a trip to the bakeshop. Transfixed, the little tot would stare, wide-eyed, at the éclairs, napoleons, and charlotte russes. Something was wrong today. He could not help but notice the tumult coming from the back of the bakery.

"Listen, Shmuel, I don't care how you made it in Leipzig. Here we use Eggomatic Sponge Mix, ZB39, and Turbo Fluff. It's cheap. It's easy. Do you think those putzes can tell the difference?"

Do you remember incidents like this? Well, probably not . . . and neither do I, but the Old World craft of professional baking was also corrupted by the invasion of the instant. Bit by bit and one by one, bakeshops adapted commercial methods. Instead of crafting fine pastries, workers eventually assembled prefabricated parts, then filled and frosted them with artificially flavored goo.

CREAM-FILLED DEVIL'S FOOD CUPCAKES

Individual devil's food cakes stuffed with vanilla cream filling are the lunch box treat that most people fondly remember. Almost everyone had a favorite: Yankee Doodles with the dot on top, Ho Ho's with the squiggle, hot dog–shaped Devil Dogs, Yodels (the miniature cake rolls), and, of course, Ring-Dings. Most of these nostalgic desserts are still around, but when was the last time that you actually had them? What would they taste like today? Would our dreams be shattered? Would they turn out to be sickening sweet concoctions of artificially flavored . . . uh, stuff. Do yourself a flavor and try this adult version. In the famous words of that poor, hungry rabbit and those rotten kids: "Tricks are for kids."

❖❖❖❖❖❖❖❖❖❖❖❖❖❖❖❖❖❖❖❖❖❖❖❖❖❖❖

FOR THE DEVIL'S FOOD CAKE
Nonstick vegetable spray for coating muffin tin
1¼ cups cake flour
½ cup unsweetened Dutch-processed cocoa powder
1 teaspoon baking soda
¼ teaspoon baking powder
½ teaspoon salt
10 tablespoons (1¼ sticks) unsalted butter at room temperature
1½ cups sugar
3 large eggs
½ cup buttermilk
1 teaspoon vanilla extract
½ cup brewed strong, hot coffee

FOR THE VANILLA CREAM FILLING
3 tablespoons vegetable shortening
3 tablespoons unsalted butter at room temperature
1 cup confectioners' sugar
1 teaspoon vanilla extract
1 cup light corn syrup

FOR THE GANACHE FROSTING
5 ounces semisweet chocolate, coarsely chopped
¾ cup heavy cream

❖❖❖❖❖❖❖❖❖❖❖❖❖❖❖❖❖❖❖❖❖❖❖❖❖❖❖

1. Make the Devil's Food Cake: Set a rack in the middle of the oven and preheat to 350°F. Generously coat a 12-slot muffin tin with nonstick vegetable spray.

2. Into a large bowl, sift the flour, cocoa, baking soda, baking powder, and salt together— three times.

3. In a mixing bowl, beat the butter and sugar together at high speed for 15 seconds, until combined. Add the eggs, one at a time, beating until each is incorporated. Continue beating until light and fluffy, about 6 minutes more.

4. With the mixer on its lowest setting, beat in a third of the flour mixture. Beat in the buttermilk and vanilla, then another third of the flour. Beat in the coffee and then the remaining flour.

5. Fill the cups of the muffin tin two-thirds full and bake for 15 minutes, or until the centers spring back when lightly pressed and a cake tester comes out clean. Set the pan on a rack to cool.

6. Make the Vanilla Cream Filling: With an electric mixer, beat together the vegetable shortening and butter until blended. Turn the mixer down to its lowest setting and gradually add the confectioners' sugar. Turn the mixer back up and beat at high speed until light and fluffy, about 5 minutes. At a drizzle, gradually beat in the vanilla and corn syrup until the filling is the consistency of mayonnaise, about 2 minutes more.

7. Scrape the Vanilla Cream Filling into a pastry bag fitted with a ¼-inch plain tip. With a small knife, carefully carve a 1-inch-round by 1-inch-deep plug out of the bottoms of the cupcakes—you're going to need the plug to refill the hole, so don't chuck it out. Fill with the vanilla cream. Cut a ¼-inch disk off the cake plug and cover the exposed cream.

8. Make the Ganache Frosting: Put the chocolate in a small bowl. In a small saucepan, over medium heat, bring the cream just to the simmering point. Pour the hot cream over the chocolate and, working from the center out, gently stir with a whisk to melt the chocolate and blend until smooth.

9. Dunk the cupcakes into the frosting to coat, then place on a rack, frosted side up. Transfer to the refrigerator for 20 minutes to set before serving.

Makes 24 large cupcakes

For a nostalgic and decorative touch (this is strictly optional): Fill a small bowl 1 inch deep with very hot water. Put 1 ounce of white chocolate in a completely dry coffee cup, then set the cup in the bowl of water. Let sit for 2 minutes, then stir until completely melted and smooth. Transfer the white chocolate to a paper cornet or pastry bag fitted with a 1⁄16-inch tip. Inscribe a squiggly line across the tops of the cupcakes. Let set.

DOUBLE-DUNK CHOCOLATE-COCONUT CUPCAKES

A good dunking in a syrupy frosting makes this already moist cake downright juicy. Then, for a layer of crunch, it takes a roll through crisp, toasted coconut.

◆◆◆◆◆◆◆◆◆◆◆◆◆◆◆◆◆◆◆◆◆◆◆◆◆◆◆◆◆

FOR THE CAKE
Nonstick vegetable spray for coating muffin tin
1¼ cups cake flour
¾ cup unsweetened Dutch-processed cocoa
¼ teaspoon baking powder
¼ teaspoon salt
½ cup (1 stick) unsalted butter at room temperature

1½ cups sugar
3 large eggs
½ cup buttermilk

FOR THE FROSTING
¾ cup hot coffee
1 tablespoon unsalted butter
½ cup cocoa
¾ cup confectioners' sugar
1½ cups unsweetened coconut flakes, toasted (page 3)

◆◆◆◆◆◆◆◆◆◆◆◆◆◆◆◆◆◆◆◆◆◆◆◆◆◆◆◆◆

1. Make the Cake: Set a rack in the middle of the oven and preheat to 350°F. Lightly coat a 12-slot muffin tin with nonstick vegetable spray.

2. Into a large bowl, sift the flour, cocoa, baking powder, and salt together—three times.

3. In a mixing bowl, beat the butter and sugar at high speed for 15 seconds, until combined. Add the eggs, one at a time, beating until each is incorporated. Continue beating until light and fluffy, about 6 more minutes. With the mixer on its lowest setting, beat in half of the flour mixture, then the buttermilk, and, finally, the other half of the flour mixture.

4. Fill the cups of the muffin tin two-thirds full with the batter. Bake for 16 minutes or until the center springs back when lightly pressed and a cake tester comes out clean. Set the pan on a rack to cool.

5. Make the Frosting: In a large bowl, whisk together the coffee, butter, cocoa, and confectioners' sugar. Remove the cupcakes from the tin. Dip them into the chocolate syrup to coat the sides thoroughly, then roll in the coconut.

Makes 12 cupcakes

Cream filled devil's food cupcake, Double-dunk chocolate-coconut cupcake, and Chocolate-chip cupcake

CHOCOLATE-CHIP CUPCAKES

Cupcakes like these were in the repertoire of almost every retro-mommie; they are the perfect after-school snack. The frosting was usually chocolate and confectioners' sugar, beaten with a vegetable shortening like Fluffo or Crisco. You may also frost them with Chocolate Ganache (page 8).

Be prepared—this is an extreme comfort food, the type you will just keep on eating. Once you start, do not attempt to operate heavy machinery, like a TV set, or recline on the sofa.

❖❖❖❖❖❖❖❖❖❖❖❖❖❖❖❖❖❖❖❖❖❖❖❖❖❖❖

FOR THE CAKE

1 recipe batter for Buttermilk Cake (page 44, steps 2–4) or Yellow Cake (page 12, steps 2–4)

1 cup (6 ounces) semisweet chocolate chips

FOR THE CHOCOLATE BUTTERCREAM

4 ounces unsweetened chocolate

½ cup (1 stick) unsalted butter at room temperature

¼ cup confectioners' sugar

2 large egg whites

¼ cup granulated sugar

❖❖❖❖❖❖❖❖❖❖❖❖❖❖❖❖❖❖❖❖❖❖❖❖❖❖❖

1. Set a rack in the middle of the oven and preheat to 350°F. Line a 12-slot muffin tin with paper or foil liners.

2. Make the Buttermilk Cake or Yellow Cake batter (steps 2–4). Fold in the chocolate chips.

3. Fill the cups of the muffin tin two-thirds full with the batter and bake for 16 minutes, or until the center springs back when lightly pressed and a cake tester comes out clean. Set the pan on a rack to cool.

4. Make the Chocolate Buttercream: Melt the chocolate in a completely dry bowl, or in the top of a double boiler, set over barely simmering water.

5. In a mixing bowl, beat the butter and confectioners' sugar until light and fluffy, about 3 minutes. Beat in the melted chocolate.

6. Put the egg whites and granulated sugar into a clean mixing bowl and set over a pan of simmering water. Whisk constantly until the mixture is the temperature of very hot bath-

water (160°F). Remove from the heat and continue to whisk (you can switch to an electric mixer) until the whites have the consistency of shaving cream, about 2 minutes. Fold the egg whites into the chocolate mixture.

7. Spread the frosting on the cupcakes with an offset spatula or transfer the frosting to a pastry bag fitted with a star tip and pipe it out.

Makes 12 cupcakes.

DESSERTS *on the* DIAL

On *The Abbott and Costello Show*, Lou was once baked into his own cake. The weird thing about it . . . it was his own idea.

CARAMEL-APPLE
CHIFFON CUPCAKES

Harry Baker, a Los Angeles insurance salesman and part-time caterer, came up with a unique way of making cakes that were "light as angel food, rich as butter cake." He served his "chiffon" cakes at Hollywood parties and sold them to the Brown Derby restaurant.

In 1947, General Mills bought the recipe and, through their cyber spokesmodel, Betty Crocker, announced "the biggest cake-making news in a century." The secret to this "luscious cake that even a beginner can produce" was simply vegetable oil. All of the hype and hoopla about chiffon cakes is true. They are incredibly moist and practically effortless to make. They can be created in a cornucopia of flavors.

❖❖❖❖❖❖❖❖❖❖❖❖❖❖❖❖❖❖❖❖❖❖❖❖❖❖

1 cup cake flour
1¼ teaspoons baking powder
¼ teaspoon plus a pinch of salt
1 cup sugar, divided
6 tablespoons vegetable oil
4 large eggs, separated
¼ cup cream sherry, such as Harvey's or Dry Sack

¼ cup frozen apple juice concentrate, thawed
Pinch of cream of tartar
3 large Granny Smith or other baking apples, peeled, cored, and cut into ½-inch chunks
Butterscotch Sauce (page 195)

❖❖❖❖❖❖❖❖❖❖❖❖❖❖❖❖❖❖❖❖❖❖❖❖❖❖

1. Set a rack in the middle of the oven and preheat to 350°F. Line a 12-slot muffin tin with large paper or foil cupcake liners.

2. Into a large mixing bowl, sift the flour, baking powder, ¼ teaspoon of the salt, and ½ cup of the sugar together—three times. Form a well in the center and add the oil, egg yolks, sherry, and apple juice concentrate. On low speed, mix together, just until blended.

3. In a clean, dry mixing bowl, whisk the egg whites with the pinches of salt and cream of tartar until creamy, foamy, and barely able to hold peaks, about 2 minutes. While sprinkling in the remaining ½ cup of sugar, whisk until the egg whites have the consistency of shaving cream.

4. Fold a third of the egg whites into the yolk mixture. Fold in the remainder of the whites. Fill the cups of the muffin tin no more than two-thirds full with the batter and top with the

apple chunks. Bake for 16 minutes, or until the center springs back when lightly pressed and a cake tester comes out clean. Cool the cupcakes on a rack.

5. When cool, drizzle with Butterscotch Sauce.

Makes 12 large cupcakes that will last for 2 days if well wrapped

CHARLOTTE RUSSE

$\mathcal{O}$*nce upon a time,* $\mathcal{F}$*rench master chef Antoine Carème created something called a charlotte russe. (It was the grandmammy of the icebox cake and looked like one of Jacqueline Kennedy's hats.) Our Charlotte Russe has nothing to do with Antoine's chapeau-shaped pudding. As a matter of fact, it doesn't even resemble a charlotte, except in the most abstract of interpretations.*

Our Charlotte Russe was a little whipped-cream cake that was stuffed into a cardboard cup with a movable bottom. You could keep pushing it up as you ate it. It was all yours to eat, play with, and enjoy.

Sponge cake was commonly used, but nothing beats the flavor of a buttermilk cake. You may also use the batter for Hot-Milk Sponge Cake (page 14, steps 2–4) or Yellow Cake (page 12, steps 2–4); the baking time remains the same.

♦♦♦♦♦♦♦♦♦♦♦♦♦♦♦♦♦♦♦♦♦♦♦♦♦♦♦

FOR THE BUTTERMILK CAKE
Nonstick vegetable spray for coating
  muffin tin
1½ cups cake flour
1 teaspoon baking powder
¼ teaspoon baking soda
¼ teaspoon salt
½ cup (1 stick) unsalted butter at room
  temperature
1 cup sugar
2 large eggs
¾ cup buttermilk
1½ teaspoons vanilla extract

FOR THE FILLING
¼ cup raspberry jam or preserves
2 tablespoons white grape juice or water
1 recipe Whipped Cream (page 196)
12 strawberries

♦♦♦♦♦♦♦♦♦♦♦♦♦♦♦♦♦♦♦♦♦♦♦♦♦♦♦

1. Make the Buttermilk Cake: Set a rack in the middle of the oven and preheat to 375°F. Generously coat the cups of a 12-slot muffin tin with nonstick vegetable spray.

2. Into a large bowl, sift the flour, baking powder, baking soda, and salt together—three times.

3. In the bowl of an electric mixer, beat the butter and sugar together, at high speed, for 15 seconds, until combined. Add the eggs, one at a time, beating until each is incorporated. Continue beating until light and fluffy, about 6 minutes more.

4. With the mixer on its lowest setting, beat in a third of the flour mixture. Beat in half of the

buttermilk and the vanilla, then another third of the flour mixture. Beat in the remaining buttermilk and then the remaining flour.

5. Fill the cups of the muffin tin two-thirds full and bake for 15 minutes, or until the centers spring back when lightly pressed and a cake tester comes out clean. Set the pan on a rack to cool.

6. Cut twelve 2¼-inch circles and twelve 2- by 8½-inch bands out of glossy card stock. Wrap the bands around the circles to form cups and secure with tape or decorative ribbon. Do not tape any part of the circle. It must remain free to move.

7. Mix the preserves and grape juice (or water) until smooth. Split the cakes into two layers. Spread a teaspoon of the preserves in between. Place the cakes in the paper holders so the cake top is even with the paper rim.

8. Fill a pastry bag fitted with a star tip with whipped cream. Pipe it to rise 1 inch above the paper rims. Top each with a strawberry.

Makes 12 cakes

This recipe may also be used to produce eight larger charlottes russes. Bake the cakes in a jumbo muffin tin. Cut the circles 3¼ inches in diameter and the bands 10½ inches long.

Charlotte russe is simplicity at its best. What an opportunity to flip things around. So, how about . . .

Chocolate Charlotte Russe
Follow the instructions above but substitute the Devil's Food Cake (page 36). The baking time will remain the same. Top with Chocolate Whipped Cream (page 196).

CHOCOLATE ÉCLAIRS

$\mathscr{W}hat\ could\ be\ a\ more\ elegant\ treat\ than\ a\ custardy,\ chocolate\ éclair?$ Pâte à choux, *the dough used for both éclairs and cream puffs, must first be cooked on the stove before baking. For a crisp and airy shell, follow instructions carefully. Take your time mixing and make sure the dough is smooth before you add the next egg.*

✦✦✦✦✦✦✦✦✦✦✦✦✦✦✦✦✦✦✦✦✦✦✦✦✦✦✦✦

FOR THE *PÂTE À CHOUX*
¾ cup water
6 tablespoons (¾ stick) unsalted butter
⅛ teaspoon salt
½ cup plus 2 tablespoons all-purpose flour
3 large eggs plus 1 more egg for the wash

FOR THE CHOCOLATE GLAZE
3 tablespoons strong brewed coffee
2 tablespoons light corn syrup
½ cup sugar
4 ounces chopped semi- or bittersweet
    chocolate
1 recipe Pastry Cream (see Vanilla
    Pudding, page 100)

✦✦✦✦✦✦✦✦✦✦✦✦✦✦✦✦✦✦✦✦✦✦✦✦✦✦✦

1. Make the *Pâte à Choux:* In a heavy medium saucepan, bring the water, butter, and salt to a boil. When the butter has completely melted, remove from the heat and add the flour. Stir vigorously with a wooden spoon until combined. Return the pan to low heat and, while constantly stirring, cook for 3 to 4 minutes. The dough is ready when it is no longer sticky and forms a soft ball that follows the spoon around the pan. Transfer the dough to a clean mixing bowl and let cool for 1 minute. With an electric mixer, beat in the 3 eggs, one at a time, until the dough is completely smooth and shiny.

2. Set a rack in the middle of the oven and preheat to 400°F. Line a cookie sheet with parchment.

3. Spoon the batter into a pastry bag fitted with a large, plain tip and pipe 4½- by 1-inch ovals onto the prepared cookie sheet. Mix the remaining egg with 1 tablespoon of water to form a wash, and paint the éclairs with it. Bake for 20 minutes, until firm and golden.

4. Turn the oven down to 300°F and transfer 1 éclair from the oven to a work surface. With a serrated knife, slice off the upper quarter and retain. Scoop out the soft interior with a teaspoon. One at a time, proceed with the rest of the éclairs in the same manner.

5. Make the Chocolate Glaze: In a small saucepan, cook the coffee, corn syrup, and sugar until all the crystals are dissolved.

6. Put the chocolate in a medium bowl and pour the hot syrup over it. Gently stir until melted and smooth.

7. While the glaze is still hot, drag the tops through it so they are coated with chocolate. Let the excess drip back into the bowl, then put on a wire rack to set, about 15 minutes.

8. Fill the éclair bottoms with Pastry Cream. Replace the tops. They're best served right away. You can refrigerate éclairs for up to 6 hours, but they may lose some crunch.

Makes 8 éclairs

If the éclair shells go soft (from humidity), pop them into a moderate (325°F) oven for 2 to 3 minutes to crisp up. You may also freeze the empty shells and revive them by baking in a preheated 350°F oven for 4 minutes.

CREAM-PUFF SWANS

Before the modern era of dramatically plated, architectural phenomena, desserts in restaurants were mostly slices of cakes or little individual pastries displayed on a fancy cart. The darling of the pastry cart was always a little cream puff that was shaped like a swan. For extra drama, the waiter might float the little critter in a pond of chocolate sauce. For an added attraction, tuck some berries or kiwi slices into the tops of your swans. For the ultimate touch, give them 2 dots of melted chocolate for the eyes.

❖❖❖❖❖❖❖❖❖❖❖❖❖❖❖❖❖❖❖❖❖❖❖❖❖❖

1 recipe *Pâte à Choux* (page 46, steps 1–3, including the egg wash)
Whipped Cream (page 196) or ice cream

Confectioners' sugar for dusting
Chocolate Fudge Sauce (page 199), Rich Chocolate Syrup (page 200), or Melba Sauce (page 124)

❖❖❖❖❖❖❖❖❖❖❖❖❖❖❖❖❖❖❖❖❖❖❖❖❖❖

1. Line a baking sheet with parchment. Fit a pastry bag with a large, plain tip. Fill with all but ¼ cup of the *Pâte à Choux*. Pipe eight 3½-inch teardrops of dough on the baking sheet.

2. Spoon the reserved ¼ cup of dough into a small pastry bag fitted with a ⅛-inch plain tip. To make the neck and head for the swan, pipe 3-inch question marks onto the lined baking sheets, starting at their bottoms and pulling the bag up at the end to form a beak.

3. Coat the teardrops and necks with egg wash and bake as for Chocolate Éclairs (page 46, step 3).

4. With a serrated knife, slice off the upper quarter of each puff. Spoon out the excess dough from the bottoms. Slice the tops down the middle to form two teardrop-shaped wings.

5. To assemble, fill the bottoms with Whipped Cream and refrigerate for up to 2 hours before serving. If you're using ice cream, you'll have to work quickly and put the puffs in the freezer for up to 30 minutes before serving. Carefully remove the necks from the baking sheet and stick them into the wide end of the body. Tuck the top halves into the sides to form wings. Dust lightly with confectioners' sugar. If desired, spoon some Chocolate Fudge Sauce, Rich Chocolate Syrup, or Melba Sauce onto individual dessert plates, so your swans will have a pond to swim around in.

Makes 8 swans

S'MORES

The S'more (*pronounced* Shmoor *in some circles*) *was reputedly invented in the early sixties by the Girl Scouts. These crisp squares are fun to make and big on flavor. How can anything so good for you taste so good? Don't be a square. Make your own graham crackers and marshmallows, then be prepared for the perfect campfire snack: melty on the inside, char-broiled on the out.*

◆◆◆◆◆◆◆◆◆◆◆◆◆◆◆◆◆◆◆◆◆◆◆◆◆◆◆◆◆

**FOR THE GRAHAM CRACKERS
(MAKES 48)**
½ cup all-purpose flour
1¼ cups whole-wheat flour
½ cup rye flour*
½ cup sugar
1 teaspoon baking powder
½ teaspoon baking soda
½ teaspoon salt
¼ teaspoon ground cinnamon
½ cup (1 stick) cold butter, cut into
   pea-size bits

2 tablespoons honey
2 tablespoons molasses
¼ cup cold water
1 teaspoon vanilla extract

TO ASSEMBLE THE S'MORES
1 recipe Marshmallows (page 184 or
   store-bought)
8 ounces semi- or bittersweet chocolate,
   in chunks or squares

◆◆◆◆◆◆◆◆◆◆◆◆◆◆◆◆◆◆◆◆◆◆◆◆◆◆◆◆

1. Make the Graham Crackers: In a food processor or the bowl of an electric mixer, mix together the all-purpose, whole-wheat, and rye flours; sugar; baking powder; baking soda; salt; and cinnamon. Add the cold butter and mix or process until the mixture resembles coarse meal. Add the honey, molasses, water, and vanilla. Mix until the dough comes together in a ball.

2. Between 2 sheets of wax paper or plastic wrap, roll the dough ½ inch thick. Chill for 1 hour, until firm.

3. Set a rack in the middle of the oven and preheat to 350°F.

4. Lightly flour the dough and roll ⅛ inch thick. With a sharp knife or cookie cutter, cut into 2-inch squares. (Yes, you may get creative and cut them any shape that you wish.) Arrange the crackers on nonstick or parchment-lined cookie sheets. With a fork, prick several holes in each cracker. Bake for 15 minutes, until lightly browned at the edges. Remove from the oven and let cool right in the pan.

*Rye flour can be found in health food stores. It is preferable to use light rye.

5. To assemble: Slowly toast a skewered marshmallow over an open fire until hot and gooey on the inside and charcoal-crusty on the outside. Quickly blow it out and sandwich it, with a piece of chocolate, between 2 graham crackers.

Makes 24 S'mores

VARIATIONS

Coconut or Pecan Grahams: For nutty graham crackers, use only 1 cup of whole-wheat flour and add ½ cup of unsweetened coconut flakes or chopped pecans.

Sloppy Sh'moes: When the weather is a bit on the inclement side, make your S'mores indoors. No, you don't have to build a campfire on your Heywood Wakefield coffee table. Just put everything together lasagna style, and bake Sloppy Joe S'mores (better known as Sloppy Sh'moes) in the oven.

1. Preheat the oven to 500°F.

2. Line a large casserole with a layer of graham crackers. Sprinkle with chopped chocolate or chocolate chips, then cover with marshmallows. Repeat process with another layer on top. Place in the oven for 6 minutes, until browned, melted, and VERY GOOEY.

CAKE CUPS

You can still find them, but packages of dish-shaped sponge cakes were once as popular as hula hoops. Picture a tart shell made of cake. Magazine articles recommended that we "[t]ake a can of . . ." to create a virtual plethora of instant fillings for them, but they were most commonly used as ersatz shortcakes.

Scour the flea markets and garage sales for little indented pans. They are perfect for cake cups. You can also use individual tart tins. They will have flat tops but will still function perfectly well.

❖❖❖❖❖❖❖❖❖❖❖❖❖❖❖❖❖❖❖❖❖❖❖❖

**Nonstick vegetable spray for coating tart
    tins
1 recipe batter for Yellow Cake (page
    12, steps 2–4) or Buttermilk Cake
    (page 44) or Hot-Milk Sponge Cake
    (page 14)**

❖❖❖❖❖❖❖❖❖❖❖❖❖❖❖❖❖❖❖❖❖❖❖❖

1. Set a rack in the middle of the oven and preheat to 350°F. Arrange eight 3-inch tart tins on a baking sheet and lightly coat them with nonstick vegetable spray.

2. Make the batter: Fill the tins half full with batter. Bake for 10 minutes, or until golden brown, the center springs back when lightly pressed, and a cake tester comes out clean. Set the baking sheet of pans on a rack to cool.

3. Remove the cakes and bake the leftover batter. You may wrap and freeze any leftover cakes for another time.

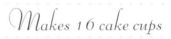

Makes 16 cake cups

> ## Whatever Happened to Baby Jane's Tomato Cake?
> The fifties saw a last-ditch attempt to revive the once popular (no kidding) tomato pastry. Back-of-the-can recipe pitches were hurled for Hunt's Tomato Sauce Cake, Campbell's Tomato Soup Cake, and "Love Apple Pie," made with Heinz ketchup.

STRAWBERRY SORT-OF SHORTCAKES

◆◆◆◆◆◆◆◆◆◆◆◆◆◆◆◆◆◆◆◆◆◆◆◆◆◆◆◆◆◆◆◆

2 pints strawberries
3 tablespoons sugar

8 Cake Cups (page 52)
1 recipe Whipped Cream (page 196)

◆◆◆◆◆◆◆◆◆◆◆◆◆◆◆◆◆◆◆◆◆◆◆◆◆◆◆◆◆◆

1. Wash, dry, and hull the strawberries. Pick out 8 perfect berries and set them aside. Slice the rest ¼ inch thick and macerate by tossing them in a bowl with the sugar. Let rest in the refrigerator for 30 minutes to exude some of their juices.

2. Divide the sliced berries among the Cake Cups. Top with Whipped Cream and 1 whole berry. Serve immediately.

Macerating is the process of soaking fruit in sugar to draw out the liquids. For a fresher, cleaner texture, we macerate some of the strawberries, then mix them with some additional fresh berries.

PEACH TARTS

· ·

◆◆◆◆◆◆◆◆◆◆◆◆◆◆◆◆◆◆◆◆◆◆◆◆◆◆◆◆◆◆◆◆◆◆◆◆

4 ripe peaches (choose freestone for
    easier pitting)
½ vanilla bean or 1 teaspoon vanilla
    extract
2 cups water
1 cup sugar

1 recipe Whipped Cream (page 196) or
    1 pint vanilla ice cream (see page 159
    for homemade recipe)
8 Cake Cups (page 52)
½ cup Melba Sauce (page 124)

◆◆◆◆◆◆◆◆◆◆◆◆◆◆◆◆◆◆◆◆◆◆◆◆◆◆◆◆◆◆◆◆◆◆◆◆

1. Slice the peaches in half around their creases. Twist the two halves and pull apart. With a spoon, pluck out the pit. Split the vanilla bean and scrape out the seeds. Reserve all.

2. In a large saucepan, bring the water, sugar, and vanilla bean pod and seeds or extract to a boil. Add the peach halves and lower to a simmer. Cook for 3 minutes, then remove from the heat. Let the peaches cool down in the syrup. When cool enough to handle, slip off the skins and return the peach halves to the syrup.

3. Drain the peaches. Place a dollop of Whipped Cream or scoop of vanilla ice cream on each Cake Cup and top with a peach half. Spoon some Melba Sauce over the peaches. Serve immediately.

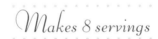
Makes 8 servings

PEAR TARTS

◆◆◆◆◆◆◆◆◆◆◆◆◆◆◆◆◆◆◆◆◆◆◆◆◆◆◆◆

4 ripe pears (Bartlett or Anjou)
½ vanilla bean or 1 teaspoon vanilla
    extract
2 cups water
1 cup sugar
1 recipe Pastry Cream (see Vanilla
    Pudding, page 100) or 1 pint vanilla
    ice cream (see page 159 for homemade
    recipe)

8 Cake Cups (page 52)
1 recipe Rich Chocolate Syrup (page 200)
    or 1 recipe Melba Sauce (page 124)

◆◆◆◆◆◆◆◆◆◆◆◆◆◆◆◆◆◆◆◆◆◆◆◆◆◆◆◆

1. Peel and core the pears. Slice them in half. Split the vanilla bean in half and scrape out the seeds. Reserve all.

2. In a large saucepan, bring the water, sugar, and vanilla bean pod and seeds or extract to a boil. Add the pear halves and lower to a simmer. Cook for 5 minutes, then remove from the heat. Let the pears cool down in the syrup.

3. Drain the pear halves. Place ¼ cup of Pastry Cream or a scoop of vanilla ice cream on each Cake Cup and top with a pear half. Spoon some Rich Chocolate Syrup or Melba Sauce over the pears.

Invest in the future: Buy U.S. savings bonds and . . . save the poaching syrup; it soaks up the flavors of the fruit and gets better every time you use it. It will last up to 1 month in the refrigerator.

When the Moon Hits Your Eye Like . . .

It was the age of the crumb crust, when making a pie dough was considered to be a tedious, time-consuming task. Besides, there were all sorts of products being hawked—in the most unusual ways. Crusts were made from Rice Krispies, cornflakes, cookies, and what have you. Fresh fruit pies were also looked upon as being old-fashioned. The most popular fillings were variations on mousse and Bavarian cream—fluffy, colorful, and often made with liquor. The flavor of booze, and generally conducting yourself like a lush, was considered to be the height of sophistication. Case in point: Dean Martin (a.k.a. Matt Helm) and his buddies in the rat pack.*

The fine art of pie throwing was invented quite some time ago, but it reached new highs . . . and lows in the early days of television. From *I Love Lucy* to *Rowan and Martin's Laugh-In,* enough whipped cream was hurled to sink a battleship, but the undisputed crown prince of pie flinging was Soupy Sales. He, or anyone in his close proximity, could get clobbered at any moment . . . and they did! Soupy even released a record album entitled *The Spy with the Pie,* in which he sang romantic strains to his "pie-faced Miss."

*Dean actually drank iced tea in front of his audience. He was a fun guy but much more interested in tomorrow morning's golf game and hanging with his kids than goofing around in nightclubs.

Some sound advice on how to bake a pie:

1. You may switch crusts around—substitute a tart shell for a pie shell. Try out different cookie crumbs: graham, chocolate, and vanilla wafer can be interchangeable, according to taste.

2. If you must, go out and get store-bought cookies or crumbs. O.K., it's extra work, but homemade cookie crumbs make a remarkably big difference in flavor. You will find recipes for all of the crumbs in the cookie section (except graham is in the pastry section). Put the cookies in a food processor and finely chop. You can also close them up in a plastic bag and crush them with a rolling pin.

Since many of the original recipes of this period contained raw egg, all recipes in this book have been reformulated to contain cooked eggs.

KEY LIME PIE

Key lime pie has been around for well over a hundred years. The originals were made with flaky piecrusts instead of the graham cracker crust that is popular today. The pie had a resurgence in the late sixties and seventies when it became the dessert darling of the "fern bars"—the raw wood and potted-plant singles' joints, where bionic hipsters and Charlie's Angels wanna-bes came to sip piña coladas and nosh on quiche.

The original pies were also unbaked. The acidity of the Key lime juice actually "cooked" the filling, almost like seviche. In today's salmonella-infested world, when an order of eggs over easy could result in a crackdown by the FBI, we bake the pie to kill off any possible marauding germs.

✦✦✦✦✦✦✦✦✦✦✦✦✦✦✦✦✦✦✦✦✦✦✦✦✦✦✦✦✦✦

FOR THE GRAHAM CRACKER CRUST
½ cup (1 stick) unsalted butter, melted
1¼ cups graham cracker crumbs
¼ cup sugar

FOR THE KEY LIME FILLING
4 large egg yolks
One 14-ounce can sweetened condensed
  milk
Grated zest of 2 Key limes
½ cup Key lime juice (about 6 to 8 limes)

✦✦✦✦✦✦✦✦✦✦✦✦✦✦✦✦✦✦✦✦✦✦✦✦✦✦✦✦

1. Make the Graham Cracker Crust: Coat a 9-inch pie plate with 1 tablespoon of the melted butter.

2. Mix the graham cracker crumbs and sugar in a medium bowl. Add the remaining melted butter and mix well. Pat the mixture evenly over the bottom and sides of the prepared pan. Chill for 15 minutes, until firm.

3. Set a rack in the middle of the oven and preheat to 350°F. Bake the pie shell for 8 to 10 minutes, until dry and solid. Set on a rack to cool. Turn the oven down to 325°F.

4. Make the Key Lime Filling: While the shell is cooling, in a medium bowl, mix together the yolks, sweetened condensed milk, and Key lime zest and juice. Pour the filling into the cooled shell and bake for 15 minutes, until just set. Set on a rack to cool, then refrigerate until chilled.

Makes one 9-inch pie or 8 servings

STRAWBERRY CHIFFON PIE

Descendants of "sissy pies," "fairy tarts," "marshmallow puddings," and "gelatin snow," chiffon pies consist of a light, ethereal fruit mousse piled high in a crust. In the forties it was almost always put in a piecrust. In the fifties and sixties, when they were often called "pouf pies," crumb crusts were more in vogue. A nice, crunchy tart shell fills the bill with the best of both worlds. O.K., it's technically incorrect to call it a pie, but how could it be wrong when it tastes so right?

Because of the uncooked meringue, the original recipe has become another victim of the salmonella frenzy, prompting new versions made with whipped cream, evaporated milk, Marshmallow Fluff, and even Cool Whip.

◆◆◆◆◆◆◆◆◆◆◆◆◆◆◆◆◆◆◆◆◆◆◆◆◆◆◆◆

FOR THE TART SHELL
1½ cups all-purpose flour
1 tablespoon sugar
½ cup (1 stick) cold unsalted butter, cut into pea-size bits
1 large egg beaten with 1 cup ice water
Nonstick vegetable spray for coating pan

FOR THE STRAWBERRY FILLING
2 pints strawberries
1¼ cups sugar, divided
2 envelopes unflavored gelatin (5 teaspoons)
1 cup heavy cream
4 large egg whites
Pinch of salt
Pinch of cream of tartar

◆◆◆◆◆◆◆◆◆◆◆◆◆◆◆◆◆◆◆◆◆◆◆◆◆◆◆◆

1. Make the Tart Shell: In a large bowl, stir the flour and sugar together. With the flat beater attachment of an electric mixer, pastry blender, or your fingertips, work the butter into the flour until it resembles coarse meal. Sprinkle in 3 or 4 tablespoons of the eggy water and mix it in until the dough comes together in a ball. On a lightly floured surface, take walnut-sized pieces of dough and, with the heel of your hand, smear them away from you in 6-inch streaks. Collect the dough and pat it into a disk. Wrap in plastic and refrigerate for 2 hours or overnight.

2. Set a rack in the middle of the oven and preheat to 400°F. Lightly coat a 9½-inch tart pan with a removable bottom with nonstick vegetable spray.

3. On a lightly floured surface, roll the dough into an 11½-inch circle. Fit the dough into the pan. Trim the dough, leaving a 1-inch overhang, and double the dough over itself to reinforce the sides. Refrigerate for 20 minutes, then freeze for at least 30 minutes.

continued

4. Line the tart shell with aluminum foil and weight down with dried beans or pie weights. Bake for 20 minutes. Remove the foil and weights. Bake for 10 minutes longer, or until lightly browned.

5. Make the Strawberry Filling: Hull, wash, and dry the strawberries. In a food processor fitted with the metal blade, puree the strawberries and ¾ cup of the sugar. You should end up with a little more than 3 cups of puree.

6. In a small bowl, soften the gelatin by stirring it into ½ cup of the strawberry puree. Set aside.

7. In a mixing bowl, whip the cream to soft peaks, about 2 minutes, and place in the refrigerator until ready to use.

8. Combine the egg whites, salt, cream of tartar, and remaining ½ cup of sugar in an immaculately clean, dry bowl and set it over a pan of slowly boiling water. Whisk until very hot to the touch (160°F), about 2 minutes. Remove the bowl from the heat and continue to whisk (you can switch to an electric mixer) until the egg whites hold soft peaks that are the consistency of shaving cream, about 2 minutes.

9. Set the bowl of gelatin over the pan of simmering water until the gelatin has dissolved, about 1 minute. Remove from the heat and mix in the strawberry puree. Let cool to tepid. Fold the strawberry-gelatin mixture into the whipped cream, then fold in a third of the egg whites. Fold in the remaining egg whites and scrape the mousse into the pie shell. Chill for at least 2 hours to set.

Makes one 9½-inch tart or 8 servings

VARIATION

Lemon Chiffon Pie: Substitute 1 cup of fresh lemon juice and ½ teaspoon of vanilla extract for the strawberry puree. Increase the sugar to ½ cup plus ¼ cup.

FRENCH CHOCOLATE SILK PIE

French fries, French dressing, French kisses—none of them come from Gaul. Although this pie has a silken chocolate texture that is "cool as a mousse," it doesn't resemble anything from Paris.

You MUST serve this pie with whipped cream and you ain't tried nothin' until you've tried chocolate silk pie and one of the chocolate whipped creams in the last chapter.

✦✦✦✦✦✦✦✦✦✦✦✦✦✦✦✦✦✦✦✦✦✦✦✦✦

8 ounces bittersweet chocolate
4 large eggs
½ cup sugar
½ cup (1 stick) unsalted butter, frozen, and cut into chunks
2 teaspoons vanilla extract
2 tablespoons Kahlúa, Grand Marnier, or cognac

One 9½-inch prebaked Tart Shell (page 60) or a 9-inch Pie Shell (page 67)
Whipped Cream (page 196), Chocolate Whipped Cream (page 196), or Fudge Swirl Whipped Cream (page 197)

✦✦✦✦✦✦✦✦✦✦✦✦✦✦✦✦✦✦✦✦✦✦✦

1. Melt the chocolate in a completely dry bowl or in the top of a double boiler set over barely simmering water. Set aside to cool down until thickened but still liquid.

2. Combine the eggs and sugar in a medium bowl or in the top of a double boiler and set over slowly boiling water. Whisk until very hot to the touch but not scrambled (160°F). Remove from the heat.

3. With an electric mixer, beat the chocolate into the egg mixture, then beat in the frozen butter for 12 full minutes, until thick and doubled in volume. Beat in the vanilla and liqueur. Scrape the filling into the tart shell and chill for 1 hour or until set. Serve with whipped cream.

Makes a 9½-inch tart or a 9-inch pie or 8 servings

> One ersatz chocolate silk pie recipe called for a crumb crust made of pulverized pretzel crumbs. We'll spare the details, but the filling wasn't much better . . . a bit more polyester than silk.

WHITE-CHOCOLATE GRASSHOPPER PIE

Way back in retro times, desserts with lots of booze in 'em were considered to be quite well bred. So, the popular grasshopper cocktail was converted into a pie. The Hiram Walker Company once suggested a grasshopper filling of crème de menthe, whipped cream, and melted marshmallows. Like its beverage forerunner, the original used a combination of crème de menthe and crème de cacao. Also, like its namesake, it tasted a bit like Vicks VapoRub and cough syrup.

We do away with the booze, substituting Peppermint Twist Sauce and/or extract and white chocolate, to create a smooth, refreshing, and scrumptious pie.

✦✦✦✦✦✦✦✦✦✦✦✦✦✦✦✦✦✦✦✦✦✦✦✦✦✦

FOR THE CHOCOLATE WAFER CRUST
6 tablespoons (¾ stick) unsalted butter, melted
30 chocolate wafers (enough to make 1½ cups crumbs)

FOR THE GRASSHOPPER FILLING
2½ ounces white chocolate
1 cup heavy cream
1 envelope unflavored gelatin (2½ teaspoons)
¼ cup milk

2 large egg yolks
2 large eggs
2 tablespoons sugar
¼ cup Peppermint Twist Sauce (page 194) or crème de menthe
½ teaspoon peppermint extract, for extra zip (optional)

FOR GARNISH
Chocolate curls or sprinkles

✦✦✦✦✦✦✦✦✦✦✦✦✦✦✦✦✦✦✦✦✦✦✦✦✦

1. Make the Chocolate Wafer Crust: Coat a 9-inch pie pan with 2 teaspoons of the butter. In a food processor, chop the chocolate wafers into fine crumbs. Transfer to a small bowl and mix in the rest of the melted butter. Pat the mixture over the bottom and sides of the pan. Chill for at least 30 minutes

2. Set a rack in the middle of the oven and preheat to 350°F. Bake the piecrust for 8 to 10 minutes, until set and dry. Place on a rack to cool.

3. Make the Grasshopper Filling: Finely chop the white chocolate and put it in a medium bowl. In a small saucepan, over medium heat, bring ½ cup of the cream just to a simmer. Pour it over the chocolate and stir with a whisk until smooth and blended. Stir in the remaining ½ cup of cream and refrigerate for 30 minutes, until completely chilled.

continued

4. In a small bowl, soften the gelatin by stirring it into the milk. Set aside.

5. Combine the yolks, eggs, and sugar in a medium bowl or the top of a double boiler and place over slowly boiling water. Whisk until very hot to the touch but not scrambled (160°F). Remove from the heat and continue to whisk (you may switch to an electric mixer) until the mixture is thick, doubled in volume, and, when tipped from a spoon, holds a ribbon shape for 2 seconds, about 2 minutes. Whisk in the Peppermint Twist Sauce and peppermint extract, if using.

6. Set the bowl of gelatin over simmering water until the gelatin has dissolved, about 1 minute; then whisk it into the egg mixture. Set aside to cool down to tepid.

7. Whip the white chocolate cream until just thickened, then fold it into the egg mixture. Scrape the filling into the pie shell and refrigerate until set, at least 2 hours or overnight.

8. Garnish with chocolate curls or sprinkles.

Makes one 9-inch pie or 8 servings

As long as it doesn't contain any filling or frosting, you can make a crumb crust from leftover devil's food cake. Follow the instructions for drying crumbs in the Chocolate Blackout Cake recipe (page 8, step 7).

NESSELRODE PIE

In the 1860s, the original charlotte Nesselrode was named in honor of a Russian diplomat. Much later on, the pudding crossed the Atlantic and landed in a pie shell. It was wildly popular throughout the Northeast. In the New York area, it was often served at seafood restaurants. Because it is fairly complicated (especially with today's raw-eggless society), it was rarely made at home. When it was, bottled Nesselrode, the marinated chestnut and candied fruit compote, was almost always used. Today, candied fruits have lost a lot of their appeal, so we substitute more flavorful dried fruits. We make no bones about it. This recipe is not as easy as pie. But, if you've got the right stuff, then take up the challenge and go for the gusto. Taste what the legend is really made of.

❖❖❖❖❖❖❖❖❖❖❖❖❖❖❖❖❖❖❖❖❖❖❖❖❖❖❖

FOR THE PIE SHELL
3 tablespoons solid vegetable shortening
1½ cups all-purpose flour
½ cup (1 stick) cold unsalted butter,
     cut into pea-size bits
2 to 3 tablespoons ice water
Nonstick vegetable spray for coating pan

**FOR THE NESSELRODE (ENOUGH FOR
2 BATCHES OF FILLING)**
One 10-ounce can whole chestnuts in
     water, drained
¼ cup water
¼ cup dark rum
¾ cup sweet Marsala
1 cup sugar
½ cup dried cherries
½ cup raisins and/or dried currants

FOR THE BAVARIAN CREAM PUDDING
1 cup milk
¾ cup sugar, divided
3 large egg yolks
1 tablespoon plus ¾ teaspoon gelatin
     (1½ envelopes)
½ cup water
2 tablespoons dark rum
1 cup heavy cream
3 large egg whites
Pinch of salt
Pinch of cream of tartar

❖❖❖❖❖❖❖❖❖❖❖❖❖❖❖❖❖❖❖❖❖❖❖❖❖❖❖

1. Make the Pie Shell: Between 2 sheets of wax paper, flatten the shortening out to ⅛-inch thickness. With a butter knife, score it into ½-inch squares. Freeze for 30 minutes, until stiff.

2. Put the flour in a large bowl. Using an electric mixer, pastry blender, or your fingertips, work in the butter until the mixture resembles coarse meal. In the same manner, mix in the shortening squares. While sprinkling in the ice water, mix with your fingers just until

the dough comes together in a ball. Pat it into a ¾-inch-thick disk. Wrap in plastic wrap and refrigerate for at least 2 hours, or overnight.

3. Set a rack in the middle of the oven and preheat to 400°F. Lightly coat a 9-inch pie pan with nonstick vegetable spray.

4. On a lightly floured surface, roll the dough into an 11½-inch circle about ⅛ inch thick. Fit it into a 9-inch pie plate. Trim the dough, leaving about a 1-inch overhang, then fold the overhang under itself and decoratively crimp it against the rim of the plate. Prick the dough all over with a fork. Freeze for 20 minutes.

5. Line the pie shell with aluminum foil and weight down with dried beans or pie weights. Bake for 15 minutes. Remove the foil with the weights and bake for 8 minutes longer, or until lightly tanned. Set on a rack to cool.

6. Make the Nesselrode: Combine the chestnuts, water, rum, Marsala, and sugar in a medium saucepan. Bring to a simmer and continue to cook over very low heat until the syrup thickens and the chestnuts are tender, about 40 minutes. Add some more water, if necessary, and break any whole chestnuts in half.

7. Coarsely chop the dried fruits and mix them in. Set aside to rest, overnight, covered but not refrigerated.

8. Make the Bavarian Cream Pudding: In a medium saucepan, over medium heat, bring the milk and ¼ cup of the sugar just to the simmering point.

9. In the meantime, combine another ¼ cup of sugar and the egg yolks in a medium bowl and whisk until just blended. While gently whisking the yolks, drizzle the hot milk mixture into them so they are gradually warmed up. Return everything to the saucepan and cook while stirring with a wooden spoon. Make sure that you are constantly scraping the spoon across the bottom of the pan so the custard does not scorch. The custard is done when it has thickened slightly and can evenly coat the back of the spoon, 2 to 3 minutes. Do not let it come to a boil.

10. Strain the custard through a fine sieve into a container and nestle it into a large bowl of ice. Let cool, stirring occasionally.

11. In a small bowl, soften the gelatin by stirring it into the water and rum. Set aside.

12. In a mixing bowl, whip the cream to soft peaks, about 2 minutes. Place in the refrigerator until ready to use.

13. Combine the egg whites, salt, cream of tartar, and remaining ¼ cup of sugar in an immaculately clean, dry bowl and set it over a pan of slowly boiling water. Whisk until very hot to the touch (160°F). Remove from the heat and continue to whisk (you can

switch to an electric mixer) until the egg whites hold soft peaks that are the consistency of shaving cream, about 2 minutes.

14. Set the bowl of gelatin over the pan of simmering water until the gelatin has dissolved, about 1 minute. Remove from the heat and mix with the custard and half of the Nesselrode (1¼ cups). Fold this gelatin mixture into the whipped cream, then fold in a third of the egg whites. Fold in the remaining egg whites. Scrape the pudding into the pie shell and refrigerate until set, at least 2 hours or overnight.

Makes one 9-inch pie or 8 servings

BRANDY ALEXANDER PIE

Here's another popular pie that was modeled after a cocktail. Once again, we've replaced the crème de cacao with white chocolate, but let's keep the brandy. In one unique version, the Knox Gelatin Company recommended mixing the booze, gelatin, and hot milk, then pureeing it in a blender with ice cubes. Try this model in a prebaked and cooled 9-inch Chocolate Wafer Crust or a Tart Shell.

❖❖❖❖❖❖❖❖❖❖❖❖❖❖❖❖❖❖❖❖❖❖❖❖❖

1 envelope unflavored gelatin
   (2½ teaspoons)
½ cup brandy
1 teaspoon vanilla extract
2 ounces white chocolate
1 cup heavy cream

3 large eggs
¼ cup sugar
Chocolate Wafer Crust (page 64) or
   a 9½-inch Tart Shell (page 60)
Whipped Cream (page 196)

❖❖❖❖❖❖❖❖❖❖❖❖❖❖❖❖❖❖❖❖❖❖❖❖❖

1. In a small bowl, soften the gelatin by stirring it into the brandy and vanilla. Set aside.

2. Finely chop the white chocolate and put it in a medium bowl. In a small saucepan, bring ½ cup of the cream just to the simmering point. Pour it over the chocolate and stir with a whisk until smooth and blended. Stir in the remainder of the cream and refrigerate for 30 minutes, until completely chilled.

3. Combine the eggs and sugar in a medium bowl or the top of a double boiler and set over slowly boiling water. Whisk until very hot to the touch but not scrambled (160°F). Remove from the heat and continue to whisk (you can switch to an electric mixer) until thick and doubled in volume, about 3 minutes. It will form a ribbon that holds on the surface for 2 seconds when poured from a spoon.

4. Set the bowl of gelatin over simmering water until the gelatin has dissolved, about 1 minute, then whisk it into the egg mixture. Set aside to cool down to tepid.

5. Whip the white chocolate cream until just thickened, then fold it into the egg mixture. Scrape the filling into the wafer crust or tart shell and refrigerate until set, at least 2 hours or overnight. It can be stored 2 to 3 days, but is best served within 24 hours. Serve with Whipped Cream.

Makes one 9½-inch tart or 8 servings

STRAWBERRY PIE (TART)

Coated in a fire-engine-red glaze (made from cornstarch, sugar, and artificial coloring), strawberry pie was a real glamour-puss, but often a disappointment. It always looked simply marvelous but was, invariably, dry and lacking in flavor. To remedy this, we borrowed two ideas from the French. First, for a little crunch, bake a tart shell instead of a pie shell. Second, plant the strawberries in a bed of pastry cream and . . . voilà! *Fifty million Frenchmen can't be wrong.*

❖❖❖❖❖❖❖❖❖❖❖❖❖❖❖❖❖❖❖❖❖❖❖❖

2½ pints strawberries
1 prebaked and cooled 9½-inch Tart Shell (page 67)
½ recipe (1 cup plus 2 tablespoons) Pastry Cream (see Vanilla Pudding, page 100)

½ cup water
2 tablespoons cornstarch
¼ cup sugar
½ cup strawberry or red currant jelly

❖❖❖❖❖❖❖❖❖❖❖❖❖❖❖❖❖❖❖❖❖❖❖❖

1. Wash, dry, and stem the strawberries.

2. Carefully remove the cooled Tart Shell from its ring by inverting it onto a plate. Flip it upright and spread a ½-inch layer of Pastry Cream in the bottom of the shell. Pick out ½ pint of the least attractive strawberries and set aside. In concentric circles, place the remaining 2 pints of whole strawberries, pointy side up, into the Pastry Cream.

3. Slice the reserved ½ pint of the least attractive strawberries. In a small saucepan, whisk together the water, cornstarch, sugar, and sliced strawberries. While stirring with the whisk, cook over medium heat until the strawberries have softened, about 5 minutes. Stir in the jelly and cook until it has melted. Drizzle the hot glaze over the berries in a nice, thick coating. Refrigerate for 30 minutes to set.

Makes one 9-½ inch tart or 8 servings

CHOCOLATE-CHERRY, PSYCHEDELIC, HAZELNUT, ROCKY ROAD PIZZA PIE

Pizza for dessert may sound wacky, but your guests will go mustang silly over this chocolate-covered lollapalooza. And talk about gooey: The topping melts together into a chocolatey, luscious, tie-dyed mess. Feel absolutely free to change the dried fruits and nuts around (dried pineapple, almonds, pecans, etc.). Here's a kooky but dandy trick for reheating without an oven: Use a hair dryer.

❖❖❖❖❖❖❖❖❖❖❖❖❖❖❖❖❖❖❖❖❖❖❖❖❖❖❖

FOR THE CHOCOLATE PIZZA CRUST

1½ cups all-purpose flour

¼ cup sugar

2 tablespoons unsweetened cocoa powder

½ cup (1 stick) unsalted butter at room temperature

1 large egg

FOR THE ROCKY ROAD PIZZA TOPPING

¼ cup dried sour cherries

¼ cup dried apricots, cut into ½-inch chunks

4 ounces semisweet chocolate, coarsely chopped

½ cup heavy cream

¼ cup hazelnuts, roasted (page 3)

1½ cups mini marshmallows or cut-up homemade Marshmallows (page 184)

❖❖❖❖❖❖❖❖❖❖❖❖❖❖❖❖❖❖❖❖❖❖❖❖❖❖❖

1. Make the Pizza Crust: Combine the flour, sugar, and cocoa in the bowl of a food processor fitted with the metal blade. With the machine on pulse, add the butter, bit by bit, and then the egg. Process until the dough is thoroughly blended and masses together.

2. Between 2 sheets of wax paper or parchment, roll the dough into an 11½-inch circle. Chill for at least 30 minutes.

3. Set a rack in the middle of the oven and preheat to 400°F. Peel off the wax paper and place the dough on a nonstick or parchment-lined cookie sheet. Prick holes all over with a fork (this is called docking). Bake for 12 minutes, until set. Place on a rack to cool.

4. Make the Rocky Road Pizza Topping: Meanwhile, combine the cherries and apricot chunks in a small saucepan and add enough water to cover. Bring to a simmer, then remove from the heat. Let cool in the liquid and drain well.

continued

5. Put the chocolate in a medium bowl. Over medium heat, bring the cream just to a simmer. Pour the hot cream over the chocolate. Working from the center out, gently stir to melt and blend until smooth. Let sit for 15 minutes to thicken.

6. Mix the drained fruit, nuts, and 1 cup of the marshmallows into the chocolate. Spread the filling over the crust and scatter the remaining ½ cup of marshmallows on top. Return to the oven to heat up for 3 or 4 minutes. Slice into wedges and serve warm. It can be stored at room temperature for up to 3 days.

Makes one 10-inch pie or 8 servings

Who ordered the chocolate and anchovies?
Just remember, you can customize this pizza with other nuts (walnuts, peanuts, cashews), dried fruits (pineapple, raisins), or even fresh fruits (raspberries, bananas, nectarines).

How about baking this chocolate pizza for the kids' next party?

GINGER PEACHY MILE-HIGH PIE

Bigger is not necessarily better. Lawsuits, dents in fenders, and pains in the . . . butter pecan, all being cases in point.

In the sixties and seventies, delis and diners touted gargantuan, but bland, concoctions of chiffon and meringue as "mile-high pies." They were the pastry counterparts of the overstuffed sandwich. The original, and genuine, mile-high pies, however, were served frozen, with light and fruity fillings and the thinnest of crumb crusts. They were full of flavor and gusto.

◆◆◆◆◆◆◆◆◆◆◆◆◆◆◆◆◆◆◆◆◆◆◆◆◆◆◆

1 tablespoon butter, melted
15 gingersnaps (enough to make ¾ cup crumbs)
One 10-ounce package individually quick frozen (IQF) peaches (no added sugar)

2 teaspoons vanilla extract
1 cup sugar, divided
1 cup heavy cream
2 large egg whites
Pinch of salt
Pinch of cream of tartar

◆◆◆◆◆◆◆◆◆◆◆◆◆◆◆◆◆◆◆◆◆◆◆◆◆◆◆

1. Lightly coat a 9-inch pie tin with the melted butter. In a food processor, chop the gingersnaps into crumbs. Spread ½ cup of the crumbs in the pan, pressing them against the bottom and sides to make them stick.

2. Partially thaw the peaches, then puree them in a food processor with the vanilla and ½ cup of the sugar.

3. Whip the cream to soft peaks.

4. Combine the egg whites, salt, cream of tartar, and remaining ½ cup of sugar in an immaculately clean, dry bowl and set it over a pan of slowly boiling water. Whisk until very hot to the touch (160°F). Remove from the heat and continue to whisk (you can switch to an electric mixer) until the egg whites hold soft peaks that are the consistency of shaving cream, about 2 minutes.

5. Fold the peach puree into the whipped cream, then fold in a third of the egg whites. Fold in the remaining egg whites and scrape the mixture into the pie shell. Sprinkle the remaining ¼ cup of gingersnap crumbs on top. Freeze until firm.

Makes one 9-inch frozen pie or 8 servings

Fruit Cocktails
for Two

oney doesn't grow on trees, and for a while, it didn't seem like fruit grew on them either. Let's face it. Who would possibly want to do something as difficult as plucking a grape or peeling an apple when you could just open a can? Thousands of recipes were developed not only for the boiled, tinny-flavored fruits but also for the goopy syrups that they were packed in. Gently poached, fresh fruits can and should be delicious.

DUTCH APPLE PIE CONES

For pie on the go, scoop this chunky apple filling into an ice cream cone. It's a low-fat answer to both pie and ice cream. It won't melt and run all over the place in the summer, and it's a nice warm-you-up treat that you can slurp on when the weather gets chilly.

❖❖❖❖❖❖❖❖❖❖❖❖❖❖❖❖❖❖❖❖❖❖❖❖❖❖

8 large baking apples, such as Granny Smith, Golden Delicious, or Northern Spy
2 tablespoons cornstarch
1 tablespoon vanilla extract
¾ cup thawed frozen apple juice concentrate

¼ cup lightly packed dark brown sugar
¼ cup dark or golden raisins
8 ice cream "sugar" cones
Whipped Cream (page 196)

❖❖❖❖❖❖❖❖❖❖❖❖❖❖❖❖❖❖❖❖❖❖❖❖❖❖

1. Preheat the oven to 400°F. Peel, core, and cut the apples into ¾-inch chunks.

2. In a medium bowl, whisk the cornstarch, vanilla extract, apple juice concentrate, and brown sugar together. Add the apples and raisins and toss. Transfer to a 2-quart baking dish.

3. Cover the dish with foil and bake for 20 minutes. Uncover and bake for 20 minutes more, stirring occasionally for even cooking. The mixture is done when the apples are just tender and the filling is clear and thickened. Set aside to cool a bit.

4. Scoop warm filling into the ice cream cones and serve, topped with Whipped Cream.

Makes 8 cones

HOT BLUEBERRY-LEMON SHORTCAKES . . . À LA MODE

With the advent of frozen biscuit dough and instant mix, all sorts of shortcakes and shortcuts became popular. It was just so easy to open a tube or a box and get creative.

Sonja Henie, the Scandinavian ice-skating star, stuffed frozen biscuit dough with chocolate to make ersatz pain au chocolat. Housewives all over the country followed American Home magazine's suggestion to "Take a can of . . ." apples, kumquats, or whatever and create instant but innovative masterpieces. So, give this brisk and delectable combination of lemon and blueberry a try.

❖❖❖❖❖❖❖❖❖❖❖❖❖❖❖❖❖❖❖❖❖❖❖❖

FOR THE BISCUITS
2 cups cake flour
¼ cup sugar
2 teaspoons baking powder
½ teaspoon salt
Grated zest and juice of 2 lemons
½ cup (1 stick) cold butter, cut into
    pea-size bits
½ cup heavy cream
2 tablespoons Demerara (crystalized,
    light brown) sugar for sprinkling on
    the biscuit tops (optional)

FOR THE BLUEBERRY FILLING
¾ cup port wine, divided
½ cup sugar
2 teaspoons vanilla extract
1 tablespoon cornstarch
2 pints blueberries
1 pint vanilla ice cream (see page 159
    for homemade)

❖❖❖❖❖❖❖❖❖❖❖❖❖❖❖❖❖❖❖❖❖❖❖❖

1. Make the Biscuits: In a large bowl, stir together the flour, sugar, baking powder, salt, and lemon zest. Using a pastry blender, the flat beater attachment on an electric mixer, or your fingertips, work in the butter until the mixture resembles coarse meal. Mix in the cream and lemon juice to form a soft dough. Knead it for about 10 seconds, then lightly flour it and pat it into a ¾-inch-thick slab. Refrigerate for at least 1 hour, until firm.

2. Set a rack in the middle of the oven and preheat to 375°F.

3. Cut out 2¼-inch round biscuits and arrange them at 2-inch intervals on a nonstick or parchment-lined cookie sheet. If necessary, gently pat the scraps together, re-chill for 10 minutes, and cut more biscuits to make a total of eight.

4. Sprinkle ½ teaspoon of Demerara sugar onto each biscuit, if desired. Bake the biscuits for 20 minutes, or until slightly tanned and springy. Set the cookie sheet on a rack to cool.

5. Make the Blueberry Filling: In a medium saucepan, boil ½ cup of the port wine and the sugar for 3 minutes to cook off the alcohol.

6. In the meantime, in a small bowl, whisk together the remaining ¼ cup port, vanilla, and cornstarch. Add it to the pot and cook until clear, about 3 more minutes. Add 1 pint of the blueberries and continue to cook until the sauce thickens and the blueberries soften, another 3 minutes.

7. To serve, split the biscuits in half. Mix the remaining pint of blueberries into the warm sauce and spoon between the biscuit halves. Scoop vanilla ice cream on the side. Wow! Serve biscuits hot from the oven or reheat.

Makes 8 servings

When it comes to cooking with port wine, the cheap domestic stuff with the screw cap is actually better than the ritzy, delicious imported stuff. A connoisseur wine tasting is one thing but when you're baking . . .

Blueberries will tell you when they are perfect. They should be deep blue, firm, and partially coated with little droplets of white wax. Soft berries taste flat. Red ones are sour. Mold is disgusting.

COCONUT–BANANA
CREAM SHORTCAKES

This is the recipe that Bob Denver needed before setting out on that infamous last voyage of the Minnow. *One day he's Maynard G. Krebs, beatnik extraordinaire on* The Many Loves of Dobie Gillis, *and the next he's "Lil' Buddy" Gilligan, reluctantly shipwrecked with Tina Louise!?!*

This is what happens when an all-star cast of nudniks gets stranded on a tropical island? You get coconuts, bananas, and a lot of inexplicably inane sitcom. Mixing a cream pie with a shortcake may sound a little strange also, but it makes mighty fine eating. So, next time you're planning a three-hour tour, this is the recipe for you.

❤❤❤❤❤❤❤❤❤❤❤❤❤❤❤❤❤❤❤❤❤❤❤❤❤

FOR THE SHORTCAKES
1¾ cups cake flour
¼ cup sugar
2 teaspoons baking powder
½ teaspoon salt
1 cup unsweetened coconut flakes
½ cup (1 stick) cold butter, cut into
    pea-size bits
1 cup heavy cream
1 teaspoon coconut extract

FOR ASSEMBLY
2 cups Pastry Cream (see Vanilla
    Pudding, page 100)
4 ripe bananas, peeled and sliced
Whipped Cream (page 196)
1 cup unsweetened coconut flakes, toasted
    (page 3)

❤❤❤❤❤❤❤❤❤❤❤❤❤❤❤❤❤❤❤❤❤❤❤❤❤

1. Make the Shortcakes: In a large bowl, stir together the flour, sugar, baking powder, salt, and coconut. Using a pastry blender, the flat beater attachment on an electric mixer, or your fingertips, work in the butter until the mixture resembles coarse meal. Mix in the cream and coconut extract to form a soft dough. Knead it for 10 seconds, then lightly flour it and pat into a ¾-inch-thick slab. Refrigerate for at least 1 hour, until firm.

2. Set a rack in the middle of the oven and preheat to 375°F.

3. Cut out 2¼-inch round biscuits and arrange them at 2-inch intervals on a nonstick or parchment-lined cookie sheet. If necessary, pat the scraps together, re-chill for 10 minutes, and cut more biscuits to make a total of eight.

4. Bake for 20 minutes, or until slightly tanned and springy. Set the cookie sheet on a rack to cool.

5. With a serrated knife, split the biscuits in half. Fill with the Pastry Cream and sliced bananas. Top with Whipped Cream and toasted coconut.

Makes 8 servings

BANANA SCHNITZELS

Call them fritters. Call them cutlets. Just don't call anybody late for dessert. These crumb-crusted schnitzels, by any other name, would taste just as good, but "schnitzel" does have a certain savoir faire ring to it. Don't you think?

❖❖❖❖❖❖❖❖❖❖❖❖❖❖❖❖❖❖❖❖❖❖❖❖❖❖

Vegetable oil for frying
¼ cup all-purpose flour
½ cup unflavored bread crumbs
1 large egg

2 tablespoons milk
4 ripe but firm bananas
¼ cup confectioners' sugar
½ teaspoon ground cinnamon

❖❖❖❖❖❖❖❖❖❖❖❖❖❖❖❖❖❖❖❖❖❖❖❖❖❖

1. In a deep fryer or skillet, add enough oil to reach a depth of at least ¾ inch and heat to 365°F.

2. Place the flour and bread crumbs on separate plates. In a medium bowl, mix together the egg and milk. Cut bananas diagonally into ¾-inch-thick slices.

3. Dredge individual pieces of banana in the flour and shake off the excess. Dip into the egg mixture to coat, then dredge in bread crumbs.

4. Working in small batches, fry the bananas for 3 minutes on each side, or until golden brown. Remove from the oil with tongs and drain well on paper towels.

5. Mix together the confectioners' sugar and cinnamon, and dust liberally on the schnitzels. Serve while still hot. Goes great with ice cream. These should be served immediately, but they can be held for 3 hours at room temperature, then reheated for 5 minutes in a 350°F oven.

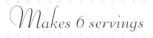

Makes 6 servings

You can also make these schnitzels with apples sliced in 1/4-inch-thick rings.

CHOCOLATE-DIPPED FROZEN BANANA BONBONS

You can serve hors d'oeuvres at the end of dinner when they are bite-size chunks of chocolate-dipped frozen bananas. They're a kiddy perennial turned into elegant bonbons. What would you give for a box of these at the movies?

❖❖❖❖❖❖❖❖❖❖❖❖❖❖❖❖❖❖❖❖❖❖❖❖❖

4 ounces semisweet chocolate
3 bananas, peeled and cut into 1-inch chunks

½ cup chopped peanuts or toasted coconut
Toothpicks

❖❖❖❖❖❖❖❖❖❖❖❖❖❖❖❖❖❖❖❖❖❖❖❖❖

1. Melt the chocolate in a completely dry bowl or in the top of a double boiler set over barely simmering water.

2. Pierce each of the banana chunks with 2 toothpicks. Dunk first into the chocolate to coat, then into the peanuts or coconut. Set on a wax paper–lined cookie sheet and freeze for 2 hours or overnight.

3. For maximum flavor, let sit at room temperature for 10 minutes before serving.

Makes 15 pieces

Try making these with chunks of pineapple in place of the bananas. Also try chopped hazelnuts, cashews, or pecans.

Double toothpicks keep the fruit chunks from sliding around.

AMBROSIA

Here's an effortless way to please a crowd on a dog-day afternoon. A simple coconut fruit salad can be a cool casserole when it has a shot of orange liqueur in it.

❖❖❖❖❖❖❖❖❖❖❖❖❖❖❖❖❖❖❖❖❖❖❖❖

3 large navel oranges
1 ripe pineapple
1 cup unsweetened coconut flakes
¼ cup sugar

¼ cup Grand Marnier or other orange liqueur
½ teaspoon vanilla extract

❖❖❖❖❖❖❖❖❖❖❖❖❖❖❖❖❖❖❖❖❖❖❖❖

With a sharp knife, peel the oranges, making sure to remove the white pith. Working over a large bowl to catch the juice, slice the segments away from the inner membranes. Peel the pineapple and quarter it. Remove and discard the inner core. Cut the flesh into bite-size pieces. Add the coconut, sugar, Grand Marnier, and vanilla, then mix well. Refrigerate and serve chilled.

Makes 8 to 12 servings

How to Test a Pineapple for Ripeness

1. Try to pick it up by one of its inner fronds. The leaf should rip right out. Experts say that this doesn't work. I have found otherwise. Regardless, proceed to step 2.

2. Grab the pineapple by its leafy coiffure and smell its bottom. The fragrance should scream, "I am a ripe pineapple." Silence indicates banal immaturity and placid flavor.

DRUNKEN WATERMELON

This was an illicit summertime treat that was very popular at college dorm parties or when someone's parents were away.

◆◆◆◆◆◆◆◆◆◆◆◆◆◆◆◆◆◆◆◆◆◆◆◆◆◆◆◆◆

1 large watermelon

1 pint plain or fruit-flavored vodka, such as Stolichnaya Strazberri

◆◆◆◆◆◆◆◆◆◆◆◆◆◆◆◆◆◆◆◆◆◆◆◆◆◆◆◆◆

Cut six 1-inch-square and 2½-inch-deep plugs in the top and sides of the watermelon. Pour vodka into each opening, then seal up with the plugs. Refrigerate for 4 hours or overnight, then slice to serve.

Serves a party

TOWERING INFERNO OF MELON BALLS

Somewhere in the sixties, the earthy-crunchy health food movement got started. Combined with the "Me, me, I'm gorgeous" movement of the nineties, it became altogether nauseating. Natural foods are downright unnatural. Humans are the only animals that actually seek out and prefer foods that don't taste good; all on the theory that if you are stoic and only eat painfully bland, disgusting food, then you will be superior to those slobs who eat junk and have all that fun....

Here's my point: Healthy can and should be tasty. Fun is good, also. So, what does this have to do with flaming melon balls? Well, this may not be a bonfire, but it is a healthy, tasty, and fun way to celebrate a birthday.

◆◆◆◆◆◆◆◆◆◆◆◆◆◆◆◆◆◆◆◆◆◆◆◆◆◆◆◆

1 large cantaloupe
1 large honeydew melon
½ small seedless watermelon
Small bunch of mint leaves or lemon
**   verbena**

Fresh lemon juice to taste
Birthday candles
Optional pansies or Johnny-jump-ups,
**   for garnish**

◆◆◆◆◆◆◆◆◆◆◆◆◆◆◆◆◆◆◆◆◆◆◆◆◆◆◆◆

1. With a melon baller (use a few of different sizes), scoop the melons into balls. You should have approximately 9 cups of melon balls. Finely chop a few of the larger mint or lemon verbena leaves. If you are using lemon verbena, remove the center stems from the leaves before chopping. Toss the leaves and balls together with the lemon juice.

2. Scoop the balls into 10-ounce pilsner or other tall, thin glasses. Push a candle into the top melon ball and garnish with mint or verbena sprigs and optional flowers.

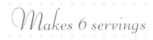

Makes 6 servings

In a vaguely similar recipe called "Watermelon Jewels," the 1972 *Family Circle Illustrated Library of Cooking* recommended entombing melon balls in raspberry-flavored gelatin.

Fruit Kabobs

Summer sun means barbecue fun, so go on a backyard food safari. Just don't leave dessert off your hunting list . . . That's where fruit kabobs come in. They can be served in the buff à la fresh fruit sushi kabobs or cooked on the backyard grill to make a berry teriyaki. Try chunks of pound cake and marshmallows. You certainly don't have to stick to the fruits suggested. Just about any combinations will do. Exact amounts are not given. This is party food. Make as many or as few as you like.

KABOBS-IN-THE-RAW

These fresh fruit kabobs are really perfect for a party. Simply skewer the fruit onto bamboo sticks. Apples, peaches, pears, and other orchard or pitted fruits must be dipped in a mild mixture of lemon and water, or they will turn brown and yucky.

◆◆◆◆◆◆◆◆◆◆◆◆◆◆◆◆◆◆◆◆◆◆◆◆◆◆◆◆◆◆

Seedless grapes
Strawberries, washed and hulled
Pineapple, skinned, cored, and chunked
Cantaloupe, honeydew, or other firm
    melons, cut into chunks

Mango, kiwi, or papaya, peeled and cut
    into chunks
Apples, peaches, pears, nectarines, or
    plums, cut into chunks

◆◆◆◆◆◆◆◆◆◆◆◆◆◆◆◆◆◆◆◆◆◆◆◆◆◆◆◆◆◆

Impale the fruit on 6-inch bamboo skewers and serve. For an exotic, luau look, serve the kabobs on ti leaves, available at florist shops.

HONOLULU HULA-STICK S'MORES

◆◆◆◆◆◆◆◆◆◆◆◆◆◆◆◆◆◆◆◆◆◆◆◆◆

6 cups mixed fresh fruit (papaya, mango, pineapple, banana), peeled and cut into chunks
½ cup light brown sugar

24 Marshmallows (page 184)
24 Coconut Grahams (page 51)
1 recipe Chocolate Fudge Sauce (page 199)

◆◆◆◆◆◆◆◆◆◆◆◆◆◆◆◆◆◆◆◆◆◆◆◆

1. Soak twenty-four 6-inch bamboo skewers in water for at least 1 hour.

2. In a medium bowl, toss the fruit together with the brown sugar.

3. In alternating order, thread the fruit and marshmallows onto 2 skewers. Grill on 1 side for a minute or two to brown, then flip and grill the other side.

4. Serve on top of a Coconut Graham and douse with Chocolate Fudge Sauce. Try these s'mores with ice cream to make a wacky Waikiki Whopper Sundae.

Makes enough for a party of twelve

BAR-B-Q-BOBS

Head for the great outdoors and create some campfire commotion with kabobs over the coals. To prevent tossin' and turnin', cut your fruit so it can be pierced with two skewers. It will make flipping the kabobs a whole lot easier.

❖❖❖❖❖❖❖❖❖❖❖❖❖❖❖❖❖❖❖❖❖❖❖

Juice of 1 lemon
2 tablespoons light brown sugar
½ teaspoon ground cinnamon
Apples, nectarines, pineapple, etc., cut
    into wedges to make 6 cups total

1 loaf pound cake, cut into 1½-inch cubes
24 marshmallows (see page 184 for
    homemade)

❖❖❖❖❖❖❖❖❖❖❖❖❖❖❖❖❖❖❖❖❖❖❖

1. Soak forty-eight 6-inch bamboo skewers in water for at least 1 hour.

2. In a medium bowl, mix together the lemon juice, brown sugar, and cinnamon. Add the fruit and toss.

3. In alternating order, thread the fruit, cake, and marshmallows onto 2 skewers. Grill on 1 side for a minute or two to brown, then flip and grill the other side. Serve hot.

Makes 24 kabobs or 12 servings

ROAST SUCKLING PINEAPPLE

A hot grill, a fat pineapple, and a bottle of maple syrup—the essential ingredients for a real New England luau.

◆◆◆◆◆◆◆◆◆◆◆◆◆◆◆◆◆◆◆◆◆◆◆◆◆◆◆◆

1 ripe pineapple
8 whole cloves
1 cup maple syrup

Ground cinnamon
¼ cup (½ stick) unsalted butter, melted

◆◆◆◆◆◆◆◆◆◆◆◆◆◆◆◆◆◆◆◆◆◆◆◆◆◆◆◆

1. With a sharp knife, remove the skin and eyes from a whole pineapple, leaving the spiky leaves intact. Replace 8 of the eyes with the cloves. Remove some of the middle leaves and center the pineapple on a spit. Cover the leaves with foil.

2. Mix together the maple syrup, cinnamon, and melted butter.

3. Rotate the pineapple over the grill, basting frequently with the maple syrup mixture, until browned and juicy and heated through, about 10 minutes.

Serves 6

How to Subdue a Pineapple—Davy Crockett–Style

Whether you're hosting a luau or flipping an upside-down cake, fresh pineapple is the way to go. Don't let the bristly critter scare you. Taming a wild pineapple is easy if you know what you're doing. Here's a very efficient and effective method, but there's more than one way to skin this varmint.

With a sharp knife, cut off the fronds and bottom (leave them on for Roast Suckling Pineapple). Stand the pineapple upright and slice off the skin. Notice that the spikes have left a pattern of small "eyes." Lay the pineapple on its side and, following the pattern, slice out these "eyes." You can remove several at a time by cutting them out in thin, narrow wedges. If the recipe calls for the pineapple to be cut into wedges, quarter the pineapple lengthwise, and cut out the pithy core. (It runs one-third of an inch along each wedge.) You may now cut your pineapple quarters into smaller wedges.

I Tawt I Taw a Pudding Tat

In 1940 the "Jell-O people" introduced their instant chocolate, butterscotch, and vanilla puddings. "Grandma used to spend an hour making that pudding of hers. . . . You can make it in minutes." Generations to come would think that pudding could be made only by opening up a little box. Nearly fifty years later, pastry chefs in fancy restaurants would wow customers by making their own "house-made" puddings.

Some Advice on Puddings

1. To help dissolve cornstarch and other thickeners, whisk them into the liquid, wait, then whisk again. Whisk it once. . . . Whisk it twice. Oh that pudding tastes so nice.

2. Slowly add hot liquids to eggs. This prevents the heartache of unsightly scrambling.

3. To prevent a skin from forming on your pudding, place a sheet of wax paper directly on the surface. To encourage a skin to form . . . don't.

CHOCOLATE PUDDING

Chocolate pudding from a package was a versatile kitchen staple: Add more milk and it could be instant chocolate sauce. Add less milk and it could be instant cake frosting. Add chocolate chips and you had the original "double" chocolate pudding.

In 1987, house-made (that means made from scratch in a restaurant) double and triple (that means a blend of high-quality chocolates was used) chocolate puddings started to appear in chic restaurants like New York's Odeon. It was the vanguard of a whole new wave of revitalized American desserts.

◆◆◆◆◆◆◆◆◆◆◆◆◆◆◆◆◆◆◆◆◆◆◆◆◆◆◆◆◆

4 ounces bittersweet chocolate
2 tablespoons unsalted butter
2 tablespoons cornstarch
¼ cup unsweetened Dutch-processed cocoa

½ cup sugar, divided
2½ cups milk, divided
1 large egg
2 large egg yolks

◆◆◆◆◆◆◆◆◆◆◆◆◆◆◆◆◆◆◆◆◆◆◆◆◆◆◆◆◆

1. Melt the chocolate and butter in a completely dry bowl or in the top of a double boiler set over barely simmering water.

2. In a medium bowl, whisk the cornstarch, cocoa, and ¼ cup of the sugar into ½ cup of the milk, then whisk in the eggs and yolks.

3. In a medium, heavy-bottomed saucepan, over medium heat, bring the remaining 2 cups milk and ¼ cup sugar just to the simmering point (it will wriggle in the pot). While constantly but gently whisking the egg mixture, drizzle the hot liquid in. Return the mixture to the saucepan and, while whisking constantly and scraping the bottom of the pan, cook until tiny bubbles boil up for 3 seconds. Remove from the heat and strain.

4. Thoroughly mix in the melted chocolate. Divide the pudding among 6 serving bowls (or pour into 1 big one). Place a sheet of wax paper directly on the surface of each to prevent a skin from forming. Let cool for 1 hour, then refrigerate until chilled.

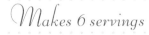

Makes 6 servings

BUTTERSCOTCH PUDDING

Everybody's got to have a gimmick and this pudding is no exception. A little bit of bourbon whiskey gives this butterscotch that extra kick.

◆◆◆◆◆◆◆◆◆◆◆◆◆◆◆◆◆◆◆◆◆◆◆◆◆◆◆◆◆

½ cup cornstarch
3 cups milk, divided
2 large eggs
2 large egg yolks

2 teaspoons vanilla extract
¾ cup lightly packed dark brown sugar
3 tablespoons unsalted butter
1 tablespoon bourbon

◆◆◆◆◆◆◆◆◆◆◆◆◆◆◆◆◆◆◆◆◆◆◆◆◆◆◆◆◆

1. In a medium bowl, whisk the cornstarch into ½ cup of the milk. Let rest for 1 minute, then whisk again. Whisk in the eggs, yolks, and vanilla.

2. In a medium saucepan, over medium heat, bring the brown sugar, butter, bourbon, and the remaining 2½ cups milk just to the simmering point (it will just start to wriggle in the pot).

3. While constantly whisking, slowly drizzle the hot liquid into the egg mixture. Return the mixture to the saucepan and, while constantly whisking and scraping the bottom of the pot, cook until tiny bubbles boil up for 10 seconds. Remove from the heat and strain.

4. Divide the pudding among 6 serving bowls (or pour into 1 big one). Place a sheet of wax paper directly on the surface of each to prevent a skin from forming. Let cool for 1 hour, then refrigerate until chilled.

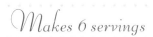

Makes 6 servings

ORANGE-BERRY TAPIOCA

Tapioca . . . How versatile are these little balls and snowflakes of cassava? They can thicken pies, be used for frozen custards, and even make a nice base for soufflés. Don't confuse the different types. "Pearl tapioca," the little "fish eyes," has to be soaked; "instant" just has to be mixed; and "quick-cooking" or granulated is in between. Here is a simple recipe for a cooked tapioca "cream."

❖❖❖❖❖❖❖❖❖❖❖❖❖❖❖❖❖❖❖❖❖❖❖❖❖

3 cups orange juice
½ cup quick-cooking tapioca
2 large eggs
½ cup sugar
1 teaspoon vanilla extract

1 cup light cream or half-and-half
1 pint mixed berries (blueberries,
    raspberries, or blackberries)

❖❖❖❖❖❖❖❖❖❖❖❖❖❖❖❖❖❖❖❖❖❖❖❖❖

1. In a heavy-bottomed, medium saucepan, over medium heat, bring the orange juice and tapioca to a simmer, stirring occasionally so the tapioca does not stick to the bottom of the pot. Turn the heat down to low and, while constantly stirring, cook for 2 more minutes.

2. In the meantime, combine the eggs and sugar in a medium bowl and whisk just to blend. While gently whisking the eggs, drizzle some of the hot tapioca into them so that they are gradually warmed up. Return everything to the saucepan and, while constantly stirring, cook until tiny bubbles boil up for 10 seconds. Mix in the vanilla and cream.

3. Divide the pudding among 6 serving bowls or pour into a 6-cup ring mold. Let cool for 1 hour, then refrigerate until chilled. (To release from a ring mold, warm the outside with a hot, wet towel or dip in hot water, then invert onto a serving platter.)

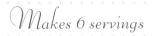

Makes 6 servings

RUM-RAISIN RICE PUDDING

If he were a pastry chef, Don Rickles, the perennial wisenheimer of stand-up comedy, could give the best advice for making rice pudding: "Keep it simple, stupid." No rice pudding recipe could be creamier, easier, or more luscious than this one.

◆◆◆◆◆◆◆◆◆◆◆◆◆◆◆◆◆◆◆◆◆◆◆◆◆◆◆◆◆

1 vanilla bean
2½ cups water
½ cup short- or medium-grain rice
¾ cup light brown sugar
1½ cups half-and-half (or use ¾ cup milk and ¾ cup cream)

½ cup golden or dark raisins
2 tablespoons Jamaican rum such as Myers's
½ teaspoon ground cinnamon

◆◆◆◆◆◆◆◆◆◆◆◆◆◆◆◆◆◆◆◆◆◆◆◆◆◆◆◆

1. Split the vanilla bean lengthwise and scrape out the seeds. Combine the seeds, pod halves, water, rice, and brown sugar in a large, covered saucepan and bring to a boil. Reduce the heat and simmer until all the liquid is absorbed, 45 minutes to 1 hour.

2. Set a rack in the middle of the oven and preheat to 300°F.

3. Remove the saucepan from the heat and stir in the half-and-half, raisins, and rum. Transfer the pudding to a 2-quart baking dish. Cover and bake for 20 minutes, until just bubbling. Let cool, then chill in the refrigerator. Dust with cinnamon. It is best served the same day but will keep, refrigerated, for up to 3 days.

Makes 8 servings

Here's a little bit of leftover magic. . . . Has last night's creamy, dreamy rice pudding transformed into Son of the Blob? Turn this sticky glob of next-day nightmare into a delectable treat. Just reconstitute the pudding by folding in some milk, half-and-half, or cream.

For some additional one-up-personship, fold in some whipped cream.

BANANA PUDDING

A descendant of the English trifle, banana pudding is a layered conglomeration of vanilla pudding, vanilla wafers, and bananas. If you want to get fancy-pants (and by all means, be my guest), serve it in a cut-crystal bowl. Personally, I think this comfort food fits better in a vintage casserole.

As for the vanilla pudding, when it's used as the filling of an éclair, it's called pastry cream. For something funky like this, it's just plain ole puddin'.

✦✦✦✦✦✦✦✦✦✦✦✦✦✦✦✦✦✦✦✦✦✦✦✦✦✦✦

FOR THE VANILLA PUDDING (PASTRY CREAM)
¼ **cup cornstarch**
2 cups milk
4 large egg yolks
½ **vanilla bean, or 1 teaspoon vanilla extract**
½ **cup sugar**
2 tablespoons unsalted butter

TO ASSEMBLE
36 Vanilla Wafers (page 156)
3½ **ripe bananas, peeled and cut into ¼-inch-thick slices**
1 recipe Whipped Cream (page 196)

✦✦✦✦✦✦✦✦✦✦✦✦✦✦✦✦✦✦✦✦✦✦✦✦✦✦

1. Make the Vanilla Pudding: In a medium bowl, whisk the cornstarch into ½ cup of the milk. Let rest for 1 minute, then whisk again. Whisk in the egg yolks.

2. Split the vanilla bean lengthwise and scrape the seeds into a medium saucepan. Add the sugar, the remaining 1½ cups of milk, and the pieces of bean pod. Slowly bring to a simmer over medium heat.

3. While constantly whisking, slowly drizzle the hot liquid into the egg mixture. Return everything to the saucepan and, while constantly whisking and scraping the bottom of the pot, cook until tiny bubbles boil up for 10 seconds. Mix in the butter. Remove from the heat and strain. Cover the surface directly with a sheet of wax paper. Set aside to cool down, then refrigerate.

4. In a 6-cup glass bowl or casserole, alternately layer the Vanilla Wafers and bananas between ¼-inch-thick schmears of pudding until you reach the top of the bowl. (To be

historically correct, the top layer should be vanilla wafer.) Reserve a few wafers for garnish and put the pudding in the refrigerator to set for at least 2 hours. To serve, top with Whipped Cream and a few crumbled wafers.

Makes 8 servings

Now, what can we do with that extra half banana? We asked our studio audience and the "survey says":

- Make half a peanut butter and banana sandwich.

- Put it in your pancakes.

- And the number one answer is: Mash it and feed it to the baby!!!

DESSERTS *on the* DIAL

What do Hogan's heroes bribe Schultz with? Strudel, of course.

CHOCOLATE-WAFER
WHIPPED CREAM ROLL

With names as vague as "cookie dessert," recipes for this "thing" could be found in cookbooks and on the backs of Nabisco cookie boxes. But what is it? A cake? A pudding? Or just some sort off yummy, creamy, delicious who's-a-ma-whatsie? You decide.

To make it, whipped cream is smeared around chocolate wafer cookies and then shaped like a pâté or meat loaf. Now here's the best part: Instead of baking it or cooking it, you just let it sit. In a few hours, it actually makes itself.

To add a little grown-up sophistication to this kiddy dessert, try flavoring the whipped cream with something exotic like orange liqueur, framboise, or mint. You may even use Chocolate Whipped Cream (page 196).

◆◆◆◆◆◆◆◆◆◆◆◆◆◆◆◆◆◆◆◆◆◆◆◆◆◆◆◆◆◆◆

2 cups heavy cream
¼ cup confectioners' sugar
**1½ teaspoons vanilla extract, or ½
    teaspoon vanilla and 2 tablespoons
    orange liqueur**

48 Chocolate Wafers (page 148)
Cocoa or cookie crumbs for dusting

◆◆◆◆◆◆◆◆◆◆◆◆◆◆◆◆◆◆◆◆◆◆◆◆◆◆◆◆◆◆

1. In a mixing bowl, whip the cream to soft peaks, about 1½ minutes. Add the confectioners' sugar and vanilla, and continue whipping until stiff but smooth, about 1 minute.

2. Spread the wafers evenly with the whipped cream and set in stacks of eight. Turn the stacks on their sides and line them up, one after the other, like the wheels on an eighteen-wheeler. Frost the top and sides with the remaining whipped cream to form a loaf. Refrigerate for at least 3 hours, until firm.

3. To serve, dust lightly with cocoa or cookie crumbs. Slice with a serrated knife dipped in hot water.

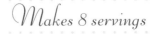

Makes 8 servings

There's always room for . . .

. . . fruit gelatin! Long before it was commonly known by one of its brand names, way before Bill Cosby sold Jell-O on TV, there was a popular dessert called fruit jelly or gelatin. (It's still called that in some places.)

Making looney cococtions with instant gelatin mixes was the ultimate form of culinary creativity. In my house, just the sight of Mom fiddling with a ring mold would strike terror into the hearts of everyone in the family. Had she read Better Homes and Gardens' advice that boiled vegetables and lemon gelatin would "taste just like Spring"? Did she see Kraft's recipe for an orange gelatin, cream cheese, and marshmallow ring?

Gelatin desserts don't have to be a box of instant this and a can of that. With fresh fruits and real flavored gelatins, they can become light dee-lites that your whole family will love.

GRAPE GELATIN

If you can't find fresh grape juice, look for kosher. Brands like Kedem have rich, full flavor.

◆◆◆◆◆◆◆◆◆◆◆◆◆◆◆◆◆◆◆◆◆◆◆◆◆◆◆◆◆

2 envelopes gelatin (5 teaspoons)   **¼ cup sugar**
4 cups Concord grape juice, divided

◆◆◆◆◆◆◆◆◆◆◆◆◆◆◆◆◆◆◆◆◆◆◆◆◆◆◆◆◆

1. In a large bowl, soften the gelatin by stirring it into ½ cup of the grape juice. Set aside.

2. In a small saucepan, bring 1½ cups of the grape juice and the sugar to a boil. Boil until the crystals have dissolved, about 1 minute. Pour it over the gelatin and stir to dissolve. Mix in the remaining 2 cups of grape juice. Pour into individual serving glasses or a 4½-cup mold. Chill for several hours until set.

Makes 4 to 6 servings

ORANGE GELATIN

....

♦ ♦

2 envelopes gelatin (5 teaspoons)   ¾ cup sugar
4 cups fresh orange juice, divided   ½ teaspoon vanilla extract

♦ ♦

1. In a large bowl, soften the gelatin by stirring it into ½ cup of the orange juice. Set aside.

2. In a small saucepan, bring 1½ cups of the orange juice and the sugar to a boil. Boil until the crystals have dissolved, about 1 minute. Pour it over the gelatin and stir to dissolve. Mix in the remaining 2 cups of orange juice and vanilla. Pour into individual serving glasses or a 4½-cup mold. Chill for several hours until set.

Makes 4 to 6 servings

Hits & Misses
The "These FOODS are NEWS!" section of a 1960 *Better Homes and Gardens* announced:

1. "All-butter, fresh-banana and fresh-orange cakes are baked, frosted, and ready to serve." They come, frozen, "in foilware pans."

2. "Chocolate-chip cookies recently made a debut as a refrigerated dough. . . . Just slice and bake."

3. "These are the newest fruit-flavored gelatin desserts . . . peach and watermelon."

In a 1956 advertisement, Jell-O bragged that its new artificial flavors could "imitate to perfection the exciting taste of sun-ripened black raspberries, the darkest, juiciest cherries on the tree, and the plump, deep-purple Concord grapes."

PEAR WOBBLER

✦✦✦✦✦✦✦✦✦✦✦✦✦✦✦✦✦✦✦✦✦✦✦✦✦✦✦✦

4 ripe pears (Bartlett or Anjou are best)
2 cups water
1½ cups sugar, divided

1 teaspoon vanilla extract
2 envelopes gelatin (5 teaspoons)
4 cups apple juice, divided

✦✦✦✦✦✦✦✦✦✦✦✦✦✦✦✦✦✦✦✦✦✦✦✦✦✦✦✦

1. Peel and core the pears. Slice them vertically into quarters.

2. In a large saucepan, bring the water and 1 cup of the sugar to a boil. Add the pears and vanilla and lower the heat to a simmer. Cook for 5 minutes, then remove from the heat. Let the pears cool down in the syrup.

3. In a large bowl, soften the gelatin by stirring it into ½ cup of the apple juice. Set aside.

4. Drain the pears and arrange them, with their cut sides facing up, on the bottom of a 2-quart ring mold.

5. In a small saucepan, bring 1½ cups of the apple juice and the remaining ½ cup of sugar to a boil. Boil until the crystals have dissolved, about 1 minute. Pour it over the gelatin and stir to dissolve. Mix in the remaining 2 cups of apple juice and gently pour the mixture over the pears. Chill the mold for several hours until set.

6. To remove, dip the mold in hot water for a few seconds and invert it onto a serving platter.

Makes one 2-quart ring mold or 8 servings

VARIATION

To turn this dish into a Peach Wriggler, substitute peach quarters for the pears. Follow the instructions for skinning and poaching peaches on page 124, step 1. Use the gelatin recipe above.

LEMON-BERRY GELATIN

Pucker up, buttercup. This lemon gelatin is quite tart. For a sweeter, lemonade flavor, increase the sugar to a full cup.

◆◆◆◆◆◆◆◆◆◆◆◆◆◆◆◆◆◆◆◆◆◆◆◆◆◆◆◆

2 envelopes gelatin (5 teaspoons)
2 cups water, divided
¾ cup sugar
2 cups fresh lemon juice

½ teaspoon vanilla extract
2 cups mixed berries (raspberries,
blackberries, and blueberries)

◆◆◆◆◆◆◆◆◆◆◆◆◆◆◆◆◆◆◆◆◆◆◆◆◆◆◆◆

1. In a large bowl, soften the gelatin by stirring it into ½ cup of the water. Set aside.

2. In a small saucepan, bring the remaining 1½ cups of water and the sugar to a boil. Boil until the crystals have dissolved, about 1 minute. Pour it over the gelatin and stir to dissolve. Mix in the lemon juice and vanilla. Stir in the berries and pour into a 6-cup mold. Chill for several hours until set.

3. To remove, dip the mold in hot water for a few seconds and invert onto a serving platter.

Makes 6 to 8 servings

FRUIT-COCKTAIL
GELATIN RING

$\mathcal{B}y$ far the $most$ $popular$ way to make a gelatin mold was to mix in a can of "fruit cocktail." Each can contained five "lovely" fruits: peaches, pears, pineapple, cherries, and grapes. You could use them in "100 fun ways," for example, as a salad with walnuts and marshmallows, served on lettuce and dressed with a "blend of mayonnaise and a little fruit cocktail syrup." Make your own cocktail by dicing and gently poaching fresh fruit.

Pick and choose your fruits from those listed. Your total should add up to approximately 3 cups.

✦✦✦✦✦✦✦✦✦✦✦✦✦✦✦✦✦✦✦✦✦✦✦✦✦✦✦

½ vanilla bean or 1 teaspoon vanilla extract

2 cups water

1 cup sugar

Pear (Bartlett and Anjou are best), peeled and cored, then cut into ½-inch chunks

Pineapple, peeled, cored, and sliced into ¼-inch thick wedges

Peach, peeled, pitted, and cut into ½-inch chunks

Nectarine, pitted and cut into ½-inch chunks

Seedless grapes, split in half

Orange segments

Cherries, pitted

Mango, peeled and cut into ½-inch chunks

1 recipe for any of the gelatins (pages 104 to 107), cooked but not chilled

✦✦✦✦✦✦✦✦✦✦✦✦✦✦✦✦✦✦✦✦✦✦✦✦✦

1. If using a vanilla bean, split it in half and scrape out the seeds. Reserve all. In a medium saucepan, bring the water, sugar, and vanilla bean pod and seeds or extract to a boil. Lower the heat to a simmer.

2. Drop in the pear and pineapple, and poach for 4 minutes. Remove with a slotted spoon and set aside.

    Drop in the peach and nectarine, and poach for 2 minutes. Remove with a slotted spoon and set aside.

    Drop in the grapes and orange segments, and poach for 1 minute. Remove with a slotted spoon and set aside.

    Drop in the cherries and poach for 2 minutes. Remove with a slotted spoon and set aside. Since they will discolor the syrup, always do them last.

continued

When you have finished, put all of the fruit back in the syrup and set aside to cool down.

Mango may be added raw.

3. Prepare your favorite gelatin. Stir in the fruits and pour into a 7-cup mold. Chill for several hours until set.

4. To remove, dip the mold in hot water for a few seconds and invert onto a serving platter.

Makes 8 servings

To peel a peach, drop it into boiling water for 30 seconds. Remove and plunge into a bath of ice water. Slice it in half around its crease, twist to separate halves, then pry out the pit with a spoon. The skin should slip off easily.

Gelatin was so popular that in 1957 gelatin envelopes were packaged in "modern, flip-top boxes," for easier access.

The Posh Nosh—
Classic Desserts of
the Fancy-Pants
Restaurants

*T*hese are the desserts that were served in ritzy, "continental" restaurants—places with romantic names like Chez Bippy, where a snazzy maître d' with a name like Mr. "Z" would greet you . . . with an outstretched palm. There was always a lovely pastry cart on display, but these places took pride in how many desserts they could set on fire. From soup to fruitcake, boozy flambéed desserts were the ultimate sign of the highfalutin.

There were also brilliant restaurants—places where the food was superlative and the setting deluxe. The pastry table at New York's Voisin included chocolate boxes filled with genoise and buttercream, gâteau St.-Honoré, éclairs, *pôts de crème,* and strawberry tarts. At La Crémaillère in Banksville, New York, Antoine Gilly produced a perfect charlotte russe. In Hollywood, you could end a meal at La Rue with fruits in kirsch and Cointreau garnished with candied orange blossoms and violets, or at Scandia, with Norwegian pancakes with ice cream and strawberries, topped with meringue and doused in a rum and cherry heering sauce. At Brennan's in New Orleans the specialty has always been bananas Foster. The Beaumont Inn in Harrodsburg, Kentucky, served chocolate sherry cake, lemon orange cake, and chess pie. Chef Henri Soulé of New York's haute cuisine mecca Le Pavillon would create a "six-foot Napoléon" as a birthday surprise for V.I.P. customers.

I heard somebody say: Flambé, baby, flambé.
Dessert Inferno.

How to Flambé

Nothing is as dramatic as flambéing a dessert right at the table, but it's not just a show. It's the best method for bringing out the flavors of fruit. Flambé should be performed on a portable Sterno burner, right in front of your guests. Look for a funky old chafing dish set at the flea market. You can always replace the sauté pan with one that looks nicer. Of course you can do the whole thing on your kitchen stove. Just invite your guests in, because watching could be the best part.

Follow these rules for a SAFE and delicious dessert. You want to look cool, confident, and debonair—something quite hard to pull off when your toupee is ablaze.

1. Get organized. Things will happen fast, so have all of your tools and ingredients ready. Use a long-handled spoon for basting and long-stemmed matches for lighting.

2. Make sure that the area is clear of anything that might catch fire. No recipe in this book includes flaming drapes.

3. Measure out the exact amount of liquor that you will need and pour it from a small pitcher. Unless you are a licensed fire-eater, never pour straight from the bottle. It's as safe as juggling swords on a roller coaster.

4. Never try to "expand" the recipe. If you have extra guests, put on an encore performance. You can also stretch the portions out by adding a piece of cake to each dessert.

5. Save your chafing dish: Stir so just the bottom of the spoon rubs against the pan.

CHERRIES JUBILEE

Two preliminary tasks must be accomplished before you can take a ride on the cherry-go-round. First, you need a contraption to pit them with. There is a wide variety available and pitting takes time but is well worth it. Second, this dish was always made with canned cherries, and an essential ingredient was the tinny syrup that they were packed in. Making a superior facsimile is simple. Just steep dried cherries in a little sugar and water. Real maraschino is an Italian cherry liqueur. It's a clear liquid usually packed in a wicker-wrapped bottle.

◆◆◆◆◆◆◆◆◆◆◆◆◆◆◆◆◆◆◆◆◆◆◆◆◆◆◆

1 cup (4 ounces) dried sour cherries
1½ cups water
¼ cup sugar
2 teaspoons vanilla extract
1 pint vanilla ice cream (see page 159 for homemade)

1 tablespoon cornstarch
½ pound fresh pitted black or Bing cherries
½ cup brandy, maraschino, or good-quality kirsch

◆◆◆◆◆◆◆◆◆◆◆◆◆◆◆◆◆◆◆◆◆◆◆◆◆◆

1. In a small saucepan, bring the dried cherries, water, sugar, and vanilla to a boil. Cook for 1 minute. Remove from the heat and set aside for 30 minutes, then drain, reserving the liquid. (May be done up to 1 day ahead.)

2. Scoop the ice cream into chilled bowls and set aside in the refrigerator.

3. In a large sauté pan, whisk together the cornstarch and reserved cherry liquid. Let rest for 15 seconds and whisk again. Place the pan on top of a portable burner set at medium-high heat and, while whisking, cook until thickened and smooth.

4. With a long-handled spoon, stir in the dried-plumped and fresh cherries. Cook for 1 more minute. Carefully pour in the brandy, maraschino, or kirsch, and let warm for a few seconds. If it does not burst into flames spontaneously, ignite with a match. Gently swirl the pan and stir until the flames die out.

5. Spoon the sauce over the ice cream and serve at once.

Makes 4 to 6 servings

BANANAS FOSTER

Mardi Gras in New Orleans, the city of hot jazz and flaming bananas. The authentic Foster is made with light rum and banana liqueur, but the deep oaky flavor of a dark Jamaican rum will be Ja-makin' your guests clamor for more. Bourbon tastes good, also.

With all due respect to Goldilocks and the Bear family, I find that a half banana is too small, a whole banana is too much, and three-quarters of a banana is just right.

❖❖❖❖❖❖❖❖❖❖❖❖❖❖❖❖❖❖❖❖❖❖❖❖❖❖❖❖❖

1 pint vanilla ice cream (see page 159 for homemade)
¼ cup (½ stick) unsalted butter
½ cup dark brown sugar
4 bananas, peeled and cut lengthwise into halves

¼ cup dark rum, preferably Jamaican, such as Myers's or Appleton's, or bourbon

❖❖❖❖❖❖❖❖❖❖❖❖❖❖❖❖❖❖❖❖❖❖❖❖❖❖❖❖❖

1. Scoop the ice cream into chilled bowls and set aside in the refrigerator.

2. In a large sauté pan, over medium-high heat, stir the butter and sugar to form a smooth syrup. Add the bananas and baste for 1 minute. Carefully pour in the rum. If it does not burst into flames spontaneously, ignite with a match. Gently swirl the pan and baste the bananas until the flames die out.

3. Place three-quarters of a banana around each ice cream scoop and spoon sauce over the top. Serve at once.

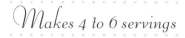

Makes 4 to 6 servings

TEQUILA BANDITO MANGOES
AND BANANAS FOSTER

❖❖❖❖❖❖❖❖❖❖❖❖❖❖❖❖❖❖❖❖❖❖❖❖❖❖

1 pint vanilla ice cream (see page 159 for
    homemade)
¼ cup (½ stick) unsalted butter
¼ cup light brown sugar
1 mango, peeled, pitted, and cut into large
    chunks

2 to 3 bananas, peeled and cut crosswise
    into quarters
¼ cup tequila
¼ cup heavy cream
Juice of 1 lime

❖❖❖❖❖❖❖❖❖❖❖❖❖❖❖❖❖❖❖❖❖❖❖❖❖❖

1. Scoop the ice cream into chilled bowls and set aside in the refrigerator.

2. In a large sauté pan, over medium-high heat, stir the butter and sugar to form a smooth
   syrup. Add the mango and baste for 1 minute. Add the bananas and baste for another
   minute. Carefully pour in the tequila and let warm for a few seconds. If it does not burst
   into flames spontaneously, ignite with a match. Gently swirl the pan and baste the
   bananas until the flames die out.

3. Add the cream and cook for 1 more minute. Add the lime juice and give everything a final
   swirl together. Place the fruit around each ice cream scoop and spoon sauce over the top.
   Serve at once.

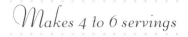
Makes 4 to 6 servings

STRAWBERRIES ROMANOFF

When he was the chef at the Carlton Hotel in London, Escoffier created Strawberries Américaine Style—strawberries in orange liqueur, blended into whipped cream and softened ice cream. Little did he know that it would one day be the star dessert of every posh dining spot in California. "Prince" Mike Romanoff "borrowed" the recipe and gave it a new moniker. Soon it was the hottest item on the West Coast. The L.A. Biltmore called it "Strawberries Biltmore." The Palace Hotel in San Francisco served it with anisette and maraschino.

All gourmets know that good cooking starts with good stock. In this case, the bouillon in question is ice cream soup. Every kid instinctively knows the recipe. Take a bowl of ice cream and smush it into obliteration. It makes a yummy mushy mess. Kitchen sophisticates, like you and I, might prefer to make our ice cream soup from scratch. If you do, just use 2 cups of vanilla ice cream straight out of the machine. You may also whip the cream with 1 cup of the chilled vanilla custard sauce (crème anglaise) that is used to make the ice cream.

❖❖❖❖❖❖❖❖❖❖❖❖❖❖❖❖❖❖❖❖❖❖❖❖❖❖❖

2 pints strawberries, washed and stemmed
¼ cup sugar
¼ cup orange liqueur, such as Grand Marnier or Cointreau

1 pint Vanilla Ice Cream (page 159)
1 cup heavy cream

❖❖❖❖❖❖❖❖❖❖❖❖❖❖❖❖❖❖❖❖❖❖❖❖❖❖❖

1. Slice the strawberries. In a large bowl, toss three-quarters of them with the sugar and orange liqueur. Refrigerate for at least 1 hour to macerate.

2. Put the ice cream in the refrigerator to soften.

3. Put the cream and half of the macerated strawberries in a cold mixing bowl. With an electric mixer, whip to soft peaks, about 2 minutes. Fold in the ice cream.

4. Distribute the cream among 6 chilled bowls. Mix the plain sliced berries with the remaining macerated berries and place on top of the cream.

Makes 6 to 8 servings

CRÊPES SUZETTE

"The fact remains—and what a shame—it's only pancakes set aflame."
— *Gourmet*, 1943

Orange versus tangerine, brandy versus Grand Marnier, Rodin versus Godzilla. There are more ways to cook Suzie's burning flapjacks than you can shake or bake a stick at. The authentic method is shrouded in a history of mystery, but what it flambés down to is this: Escoffier cooked a prototype, but it is unclear whether he used orange, tangerine, or even a little lemon. John D. Rockefeller's chef, Henri Charpentier, started the craze of flambéing them and turned the dessert into an American classic.

Many recipes call for rubbing sugar cubes on orange skins to remove the oils, then making an orange butter and schmearing it on the crêpes. We've adapted a few shortcuts, but the final outcome is still genuine and spectacular and C.C. (culinarily correct).

◆◆◆◆◆◆◆◆◆◆◆◆◆◆◆◆◆◆◆◆◆◆◆◆◆◆◆◆◆◆

FOR THE CRÊPES
½ cup water
½ cup milk
1 cup all-purpose flour
1 tablespoon sugar
¼ teaspoon salt
2 large eggs
2 tablespoons melted butter
Nonstick vegetable spray for coating pan

FOR THE SAUCE
½ cup sugar
2 oranges or 3 tangerines
½ cup (1 stick) unsalted butter
¾ cup Grand Marnier, Cointreau, or curaçao

Whipped Cream (page 196; optional)

◆◆◆◆◆◆◆◆◆◆◆◆◆◆◆◆◆◆◆◆◆◆◆◆◆◆◆◆◆◆

1. Make the Crêpes: Combine all of the ingredients except the butter and nonstick spray in a food processor or blender and process until smooth, about 10 seconds. If necessary, scrape down any solids that stick to the sides. Add the butter and process for a few more seconds to blend. Refrigerate, covered, for at least 2 hours or overnight.

2. Set a 7-inch, nonstick crêpe pan over moderately high heat, then spray with nonstick vegetable spray. When nice and hot, remove the pan from the heat and add 2 tablespoons of batter, swirling to coat the bottom of the pan. Cook for 1½ minutes, until lightly browned. Starting at the edge closest to you, flip the crêpe over with a rubber spatula. (Use your fingers if you're brave. It really doesn't hurt.) Cook for another minute, until spotty brown. Transfer to a plate and continue with the rest of the batter.

continued

3. Put the sugar in a bowl and grate the zest of the orange into it. With the back of a large spoon, rub the zest into the sugar until it is bright orange. Squeeze and strain in ½ cup of orange juice.

4. Set a large sauté pan over medium-high heat. Melt the butter and orange-sugar mixture to bubbling. One by one, place the pancakes in the pan, folding each into quarters. Carefully pour in the orange liqueur and let warm for a few seconds. If it does not burst into flames spontaneously, ignite with a match. Gently swirl the pan and baste the crêpes until the flames die out. Serve at once. Two to three crêpes are a nice size portion. A large dollop of Whipped Cream makes a perfect accompaniment.

Makes 16 crêpes

DESSERTS *on the* DIAL

When Mike and Carol Brady's grandparents were set up on a potentially romantic date, Alice served crêpes suzette, and they burned for an entire scene.

Who played the old codgers? you ask. Heavily made up Robert Reed and Florence Henderson, who else?

Are you having trouble turning those crêpes? Try twitching your nose; your pancakes could flip by themselves. That's how Samantha did it on *Bewitched*.

BAKED ALASKA

Baked Alaska is one of those retro desserts that has had a revival in upper-crusty restaurants. Unfortunately, many of them are half-baked Alaskas: cake and ice cream with a glob of propane-torched meringue on top. Sorry, vice-pastry chef, but I knew baked Alaska . . .

Plan your strategy beforehand so you can move quickly. The ice cream must be rock hard and frozen stiff. Shape homemade ice cream by freezing it in a plastic "take-out" container. You may also use store-bought ice cream. Cut the container to remove it from the ice cream. You will have to trim the cake to fit around it.

◆◆◆◆◆◆◆◆◆◆◆◆◆◆◆◆◆◆◆◆◆◆◆◆◆◆◆◆◆◆◆

FOR THE STRAWBERRY SAUCE
1 pint strawberries, washed and hulled
¼ cup sugar

FOR THE CAKE
Nonstick vegetable spray for coating pan
1 recipe batter for Yellow Cake (page 12, steps 2–4) or Buttermilk Cake (page 44, steps 2–4)
¼ cup orange liqueur, such as Grand Marnier
1 pint ice cream frozen in a 2-cup plastic take-out container

FOR THE ITALIAN MERINGUE
¼ cup water
½ cup light corn syrup
¾ cup sugar
5 large egg whites
¼ teaspoon salt
Pinch of cream of tartar

TO ASSEMBLE
½ eggshell, thoroughly washed
1 tablespoon confectioners' sugar
¼ cup white rum, 151 rum, or brandy

◆◆◆◆◆◆◆◆◆◆◆◆◆◆◆◆◆◆◆◆◆◆◆◆◆◆◆◆◆◆◆

1. Make the Strawberry Sauce: In a food processor, puree the strawberries and sugar until liquefied.

2. Make the Cake: Lightly coat a 10½- by 15½-inch jelly roll pan with nonstick vegetable spray. Add the batter to the pan and bake for 13 to 15 minutes, until lightly tanned and springy. Set on a rack to cool.

3. Cut out 2 circles of cake, one 6 inches in diameter, the other 4¼ inches in diameter. Cut out a rectangle 3 by 15½ inches. Don't eat the scraps yet! Sprinkle the cake with the orange liqueur.

4. Wrap the ice cream container in a hot towel to loosen it. Invert the container onto the larger cake circle. Remove the container. Top the ice cream with the smaller circle. Use the

cake rectangle to wrap the sides, making sure that the wet side of the cake is facing in. Fill any gap with leftover scraps. Return the cake to the freezer. Eat any remaining scraps now. Set a rack toward the bottom of the oven with plenty of room above it. Preheat the oven to 450°F.

5. Make the Italian Meringue: Combine the water, corn syrup, and sugar in a small saucepan fitted with a candy thermometer. Over high heat, bring the temperature to 246°F (firm ball). In the meantime, in a completely clean, dry mixing bowl, with an electric mixer, whisk the egg whites, salt, and cream of tartar until creamy, foamy, and barely able to hold very soft peaks. With the mixer running on slow, carefully drizzle in the hot syrup. Continue to whisk on high until the mixture is the consistency of shaving cream, slightly glossy, and able to hold soft peaks, about 2 minutes.

6. Set the cake on a heatproof serving platter. With a metal spatula, spread the meringue entirely around the cake. With a pastry bag fitted with a star tip, pipe any leftover meringue in a decorative pattern. Pipe 1 large rosette on top and plant the eggshell in it. Dust the meringue with the confectioners' sugar. Bake for 2 to 3 minutes, until lightly tanned.

7. In the meantime, gently warm the rum or brandy in a small saucepan.

8. Pour the strawberry sauce around the bottom of the platter. Pour some of the warmed rum into the eggshell and drizzle the rest over the cake. Ignite!!!!

Serves 6 to 8

VARIATION

Baked Alaska Pie

Here is a much simpler way to serve baked Alaska: Spoon ice cream into a prebaked and chilled crumb crust. Freeze until hard, then top with meringue and a clean eggshell. Follow the above instructions for ignition.

One-fifty-one rum does not require heating. It will ignite at room temperature.

PEACH MELBA

. . . .

Master chef of all master chefs Georges Auguste Escoffier was responsible for almost every culinary innovation except microwavable popcorn. He dedicated pêche Melba *to opera star Nellie Melba.*

In the forties and fifties, cornstarch was the most popular thickening agent for the raspberry sauce that coated the poached peach half, but the ritzier versions used red currant jelly or raspberry preserves. For a touch of elegance, try a spot of booze—fancy French booze like framboise or Grand Marnier.

◆◆◆◆◆◆◆◆◆◆◆◆◆◆◆◆◆◆◆◆◆◆◆◆◆◆◆◆◆◆

FOR THE POACHED PEACHES
1 vanilla bean
2 cups water
1 cup sugar
3 large, ripe freestone peaches

FOR THE MELBA SAUCE
2 tablespoons water
2 tablespoons sugar
2 pints fresh raspberries or one 12-ounce package of individually quick frozen (IQF) raspberries
½ cup raspberry preserves
1 tablespoon framboise (raspberry eau-de-vie) or orange liqueur, such as Grand Marnier (optional)
Vanilla ice cream (see page 159 for homemade)

◆◆◆◆◆◆◆◆◆◆◆◆◆◆◆◆◆◆◆◆◆◆◆◆◆◆◆◆◆◆

1. Make the Poached Peaches: Split the vanilla bean lengthwise and scrape out the seeds. Reserve all. In a medium saucepan, combine the pod halves, seeds, water, and sugar. Bring to a simmer over medium heat and cook for 5 minutes. Slice the peaches around their creases and twist to separate them into halves. With a spoon, pry out the pits. Add the peaches to the simmering syrup and cover them with a paper towel. (Lightly immerse the paper towel so it soaks up some syrup. This prevents the top of the peaches from discoloring.) Poach the peaches in the simmering liquid for 5 minutes, then turn off the heat and let cool in the syrup. When cool enough to handle, remove the skins, return to the syrup, and refrigerate.

2. Make the Melba Sauce: Combine the water, sugar, and raspberries in a covered saucepan and bring to a boil over low heat. Simmer for 2 minutes, until the berries soften and start to fall apart. Stir in the preserves and cook until melted and combined. Stir in the framboise, if desired. Strain through a fine sieve and set aside to cool.

3. To serve, place a scoop of ice cream in a chilled bowl. Top with a drained peach half and coat with Melba Sauce.

Makes 6 servings

BELGIAN WAFFLES

A young brat, who shall remain unnamed, was presented with two great opportunities when his big brother was conscripted into taking him to the 1964 World's Fair in Flushing Meadow, New York. The first, of course, was to drive said big brother nuts. The other was to spend all of his lunch money on Belgian waffles smothered in whipped cream and strawberries.

Classic Belgian waffles are big round affairs, but don't worry if you only have the means to make the square variety. A waffle by any other name . . . Some recipes call for yeast leavening, and others, like the one that humorist Mort Sahl used to whip up for Washington glitterati, expand because of whipped egg whites. Sure, you can also buy frozen waffles, but our recipe is almost easier than opening a package. Besides, electric waffle irons are inexpensive and almost always on sale.

To help them hold their crunchy status, keep waffles in a 300°F oven while you make the rest of the batch. You may also use this method if they need a quick recrisping.

Before you start, remember: DON'T OVERMIX THE BATTER. Overworked batter will result in dense, rubbery waffles. Mix your dry ingredients thoroughly, then mix in wet ingredients until barely combined. You should have plenty of lumps in your batter. Don't worry, they will cook out.

❖❖❖❖❖❖❖❖❖❖❖❖❖❖❖❖❖❖❖❖❖❖❖❖❖❖❖

2 cups cake flour
1 tablespoon baking powder
¼ teaspoon baking soda
¼ teaspoon salt
¼ cup granulated sugar
½ cup buttermilk
1 cup milk
2 large eggs

¼ cup melted unsalted butter
Nonstick vegetable spray for coating
   waffle iron
Confectioners' sugar
Fresh berries
Whipped Cream (page 196)
Ice cream (optional)

❖❖❖❖❖❖❖❖❖❖❖❖❖❖❖❖❖❖❖❖❖❖❖❖❖❖❖

1. Preheat a waffle iron.

2. In a large bowl, stir together the flour, baking powder, baking soda, salt, and sugar. Make a well in the center and add the buttermilk, milk, eggs, and melted butter. Mix together just until combined. The batter should look a little lumpy.

continued

3. Spray the waffle iron with the nonstick vegetable spray. Blob onto the grids ¼ cup of batter or the amount recommended by the waffle-iron maker, and bake as directed by the aforesaid manufacturer.

4. Dust with confectioners' sugar and top with fresh berries and Whipped Cream. Serve hot off the griddle. If you are thinking about serving these waffles with ice cream, then go ahead. It's a brilliant idea.

Makes 8 waffles

Use nonstick vegetable spray even if you have a nonstick surface on your waffle iron. Your waffles will have a crunchier texture and release more easily.

LET'S HAVE
A FONDUE PARTY!!!

Whether your guests are single and ready to mingle or a bunch of old fogies who need a nudge to budge, nothing gets a party going like fondue. And nothing keeps it going like fondue for dessert. Chocolate sauces are finicky and can easily break if overheated. The safest way to handle them is to prepare them ahead, then carefully reheat them over a hot water bath. The flame of a votive candle will maintain a safe temperature. Sterno is just too hot. Offer a mix-and-match grab bag of dunkables. An exciting idea is to change the sauce in midstream.

The basic principles are very simple. Check out the lists below, then . . .

✦✦✦✦✦✦✦✦✦✦✦✦✦✦✦✦✦✦✦✦✦✦✦✦✦✦✦✦✦✦✦

CHUNKS FOR DUNKING

Mango, banana, pineapple, and papaya, peeled and cut into ¾-inch (bite-size) chunks

Whole, stemmed strawberries

Starfruit (carambola) or kiwi, cut into ¼-inch-thick slices

Pear, apple, peach, or nectarine chunks, dipped in acidulated (lemony) water, then dried off

Plain or chocolate pound cake (or buttermilk cake), cut into ¾-inch cubes

Marshmallows

Cookies

FONDUE SAUCES

Chocolate Fudge Sauce (page 199)

Rich Chocolate Syrup (page 200)

Butterscotch Sauce (page 195)

Hot White-Chocolate Fudge Sauce (page 201)

Melba Sauce (page 124)

CRUNCHY TOPPINGS

Toasted coconut

Finely chopped nuts

Pecan-Cornflake Crackle (page 132)

✦✦✦✦✦✦✦✦✦✦✦✦✦✦✦✦✦✦✦✦✦✦✦✦✦✦✦✦✦✦✦

1. Assemble an eye-appealing smorgasbord of chunks. Plan to serve 8 to 10 pieces per person.

2. In a fondue set, heated just with a votive candle, warm up some of the sauces from the list of dunks. Each will serve around six.

3. Set up a bowl or two of toppings. Plan on 1 cup per 6 people.

continued

4. You are now ready to proceed. For example:

You put your fork in the pound cake
You put your pound cake in the chocolate sauce
You dip it in the coconut, and you shake it all about . . .

If you have any inclination to do the hokey-pokey, please remember to turn yourself around because that's what it's all about.

DESSERTS *on the* DIAL

While trying to make Napoleons for dessert, Samantha's warlock uncle Arthur accidentally zapped up Napoleon himself. Larry tried to recruit him for a detergent commercial.

At a brunch hosted by TV commentator Ben Grauer, the desserts consisted of crêpes flambéed with orange maple sauce, orange slices, and coconut flakes in curaçao and brandied pears. The guests included Kitty Carlisle and Moss Hart.

PECAN-CORNFLAKE CRACKLE

◆◆◆◆◆◆◆◆◆◆◆◆◆◆◆◆◆◆◆◆◆◆◆◆◆◆◆◆

Nonstick vegetable spray
2 tablespoons water
½ cup sugar

½ cup pecan pieces, toasted (page 3)
½ cup cornflake crumbs

◆◆◆◆◆◆◆◆◆◆◆◆◆◆◆◆◆◆◆◆◆◆◆◆◆◆◆◆

1. Lightly grease a cookie sheet with nonstick vegetable spray. Set aside.

2. In a small saucepan, cook the water and sugar over high heat until the liquid has a golden caramel color, about 7 minutes. Remove from the heat and carefully stir in the pecans. Pour onto the prepared cookie sheet. When completely cooled down and hardened, chop in a food processor to the consistency of fish-tank gravel. Mix in cornflake crumbs.

Warning: Caramel burns; use extreme caution.

And They Could Also Bake!

Guide to the Dessert Recipes *of the Hollywood Stars*

I wouldn't be surprised if nine out of ten Hollywood stars have at some time waited on tables. This is not to say that they might know the first thing about dessert making or, for that matter, where the fork and spoon go. Then again, despite dozens of roles on the silver screen, how many show even the slightest aptitude for acting? Some, on the other hand, like Fred MacMurray, could play the saxophone, perform brilliantly in comedy and dramatic roles, and bake their own brioche. Here are some of the signature recipes that, in some circles, really made these stars famous.

Jack *Dragnet* Webb—Lemon Chiffon Pie

Barbara *Big Valley* Stanwyck—Jet Cake (spiced raisin cake with mocha frosting)

Doris *Pillow Talk* Day—Peach Angel Food Cake

Marlene *Boys in the Back Room* Dietrich—Chocolate Soufflé

Petula "Don't Sleep in the Subway" Clark—Pots de Crème au Chocolat

Cyril *Captain Hook* Ritchard—English Trifle

Shirley *Hazel* Booth—Lemon Chiffon Pie

Fred *My Three Sons* MacMurray—Chocolate Fudge Upside-down Cake (impressive, huh?)

Jerry "Formerly of Martin and" Lewis—Vinegar Cake

Mary *Peter Pan* Martin—Lemon-Lime Bali Hai, Lime Sherbet

Jimmy "Ink-a-Dinka-Doo" Durante—Custard

Dinah "See the U.S.A. in Your Chevrolet" Shore—Chocolate Chip–Walnut Pie

Deborah "John Derek's First wife" Paget—Plum Pudding

Hermione *Bell, Book & Candle* Gingold—Seedless Grape Dessert

Tennessee Ernie "16 Ton" Ford—Applesauce Cake

Don *Cocoon* Ameche—Orange Balls

Lloyd Nolan—Almond Ice-Box Cake

John "The B-Movie *Dracula*" Carradine—Washington Apple Pie

Humphrey "Here's lookin' at ya, kid" Bogart—Cocoanut [sic] Spanish Cream

Ed "Really Big Shew" Sullivan—Meringue Bread Pudding

Andy "Hey, Wild Bill, Wait for Me" Devine—Brandied Peaches

Ed "Kookie" Byrnes was famous for parking cars, combing his hair, and eating his mother's cookies. He couldn't bake.

And now, the envelope, please. . . . The winner of Hollywood's worst dessert recipe . . . and probably the way he became Ironsides . . . is Raymond *Perry Mason* Burr, for Chocolate Mousse made by mixing a jar of fudge sauce with a bucket of Cool Whip. And the Lifetime Bad Recipe Award goes to . . . Oi, I'm plotzing!! . . . Barbra "Second-hand Yentl" Streisand for Instant Coffee Ice Cream (made with melted marshmallows—could you believe?).

In *Jailhouse Rock,* Elvis stayed true to form. He passed up lunch at Romanoff's for burgers at a roadside stand.

Cookie, Cookie, Lend Me Your Comb

When Nabisco introduced prepackaged cookies in 1870, their popularity took off like Yuri Gagarin. But, in the fifties and sixties, cookie baking at home was still the made-from-scratch holdout. Oddly, this was one case where advertising and promotional recipes were often the voice of good taste and creativity. Gold Medal flour gave out recipes for scrumptious numbers like "New! Easy, Homemade Chocolate Chip Brownies" made with oatmeal and topped with an orange glaze. On the other hand, the voice of the people, in church and civic cookbooks, sounded like a silly symphony. From potato chip drops to cornflake macaroons, these fund-raising cookbooks contained some of the wildest recipes this side of *The Ernie Kovacs Show.*

DON'T BE A COOKIE NEBBISH. FOLLOW THESE SIMPLE RULES.

1. A small ice cream scoop is great for forming drop cookies.

2. Arrange cookies in an orderly fashion on the cookie sheet. Staggered lines will conserve room and help prevent cookies from "marrying" each other as they spread.

3. Roll sticky dough between sheets of wax paper.

4. Always cool down cookie pans before reusing. Don't plop dough onto a hot pan; the butter will melt out before the cookies set in the oven.

5. Even with today's Sputnik-aged appliances, no oven is perfect. Halfway through baking, turn your pans, back to front, for even baking.

6. Let your cookies cool on the pan. Don't fiddle around with them until they are cooled down and set. That could be the way the cookie really crumbles.

7. Feel free to change the size of cookies—bigger, smaller, different shapes. Just keep an eye on how they are doing in the oven.

8. To help hold their shapes, always chill shaped cookies just before baking.

LEMON BARS

It's a cookie. It's a tart. It's what happens when zingy, tangy lemons meet the incredible, edible egg, and all on a delicate cookie crust. When it comes to bar cookies, these lemon gems give brownies a tangy run for their money. In one of his trademark songs, Trini Lopez proclaimed that the lemon had a fabulous aroma but was "impossible to eat." He obviously never tried these lemon bars.

✦✦✦✦✦✦✦✦✦✦✦✦✦✦✦✦✦✦✦✦✦✦✦✦✦✦✦

FOR THE CRUST
Nonstick vegetable spray for coating pan
1 cup all-purpose flour
¼ cup confectioners' sugar
½ cup (1 stick) unsalted butter at room temperature

FOR THE FILLING
1 cup sugar
¼ cup all-purpose flour
4 large eggs
Zest and juice of 4 lemons (should make ½ cup juice)
½ teaspoon vanilla extract
Confectioners' sugar for coating

✦✦✦✦✦✦✦✦✦✦✦✦✦✦✦✦✦✦✦✦✦✦✦✦✦✦

1. Make the Crust: Lightly coat a 9- by 9-inch or 7¼- by 11¼-inch baking pan with nonstick vegetable spray.

2. In a mixing bowl or food processor, mix together the flour, sugar, and butter until it just forms into a dough. Lightly pat it over the bottom of the pan, making sure that it clings ¼ inch up the sides. With a fork, prick little holes in the dough. (This is called docking.) Refrigerate for 1 hour, until firm.

3. Set a rack in the middle of the oven and preheat to 375°F. Bake the crust for 15 minutes, until lightly tanned and set.

4. In the meantime, make the Filling: In a medium bowl, combine the sugar and flour. Beat in the eggs, then the lemon zest, juice, and vanilla.

5. Pour the filling over the crust and bake for 15 minutes, until set. Set the pan on a rack to cool. Lightly dust with confectioners' sugar. Cut into 2-inch pieces.

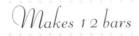
Makes 12 bars

DREAM BARS

The Great Balantine was a magician whose tricks never quite worked out as planned but, eventually, would somehow work out better. It's the same deal with Dream Bars or, as they were often called, Magic Bars. You add the ingredients in layers and . . . Presto, they bake in layers. Not very tricky, until you bite into them and . . . Presto! Change-o! Abracadabra! They're delectable.

◆◆◆◆◆◆◆◆◆◆◆◆◆◆◆◆◆◆◆◆◆◆◆◆◆◆◆◆◆◆

Nonstick vegetable spray for coating foil

FOR THE STREUSEL
1 cup all-purpose flour
½ cup light brown sugar
1 cup coarsely chopped toasted pecans
6 tablespoons unsalted butter at room temperature

FOR THE CAKEY PART
3 large eggs
½ cup light brown sugar
1 teaspoon vanilla extract
½ cup all-purpose flour
½ teaspoon baking powder
¼ teaspoon salt
1½ cups unsweetened coconut flakes
One 14-ounce can sweetened condensed milk

◆◆◆◆◆◆◆◆◆◆◆◆◆◆◆◆◆◆◆◆◆◆◆◆◆◆◆◆◆◆

1. Line a 9- by 13-inch baking pan with foil so that it covers the bottom and overhangs 2 sides by at least 1 inch. Tuck the overlap around the outside of the pan. Coat with nonstick vegetable spray. Set a rack in the middle of the oven and preheat to 350°F.

2. Make the Streusel: In a medium bowl, combine the flour, brown sugar, and pecans. Work in the butter, rubbing and pinching it between your fingertips, until the mixture looks mealy and lumpy. Lightly pat the streusel onto the bottom of the pan.

3. Make the Cakey Part: In a mixing bowl, beat together the eggs and brown sugar until doubled in volume. Beat in the vanilla extract. In another bowl, sift together the flour, baking powder, and salt, then beat into the egg mixture. Spread on top of the streusel.

4. Sprinkle on the coconut, then drizzle on the sweetened condensed milk. Bake for 15 minutes, until the first tiny bubbles come up. Set on a rack to cool.

5. When set, run a knife around the two unfoiled pan sides to loosen, then lift the whole cake out of the pan. Cut into 2-inch bars.

Makes twenty-four 2-inch bars

Lemon bars, Dream bars, and Heavenly hash brownies

From protest march to be-in, Heavenly Hash Brownies are a far-out treat for any happening. Try them tonight. Everyone in your crash pad will shout Sock it to me, baby!

HEAVENLY
HASH BROWNIES

Rocky Road, Heavenly Hash, what's the difference? *Scholars have now pondered this question for a good part of two centuries. Until proven otherwise, they can only be considered one and the same mixture of chocolate, marshmallow, and nuts. Go freak out and try any type of nut that you groove on: hazelnuts, cashews, pecans, or the original nut used in the Chunky—Brazil.*

These brownies do not contain any of the ingredients that made Alice B. Toklas's recipe so infamous. The melted and caramelized marshmallows will, however, blow your mind. Brownies are best when they're moist and chewy. These go one better . . . they're sticky and gooey.

◆◆◆◆◆◆◆◆◆◆◆◆◆◆◆◆◆◆◆◆◆◆◆◆◆◆◆

7 ounces bittersweet chocolate
¾ cup (1½ sticks) unsalted butter
Nonstick vegetable spray for coating pan
3 large eggs
1 cup granulated sugar
½ cup lightly packed dark brown sugar
2 tablespoons dark corn syrup
1 cup cake flour

1 teaspoon baking powder
¼ teaspoon salt
1 cup unsalted nuts
1 cup cut-up Marshmallows
    (¾-inch chunks) (page 184), or
    ¾ of an 8-ounce package of mini
    marshmallows

◆◆◆◆◆◆◆◆◆◆◆◆◆◆◆◆◆◆◆◆◆◆◆◆◆◆◆

1. Melt the chocolate and butter in a completely dry bowl or in the top of a double boiler set over barely simmering water.

2. Set a rack in the middle of the oven and preheat to 350°F. Coat a 9- by 13-inch baking pan with nonstick vegetable spray.

3. In a large bowl, mix together the eggs, granulated sugar, brown sugar, and corn syrup until blended. Mix in the chocolate mixture.

4. In another bowl, stir the flour, baking powder, and salt together with a fork. Mix it into the eggy mixture. Stir in the nuts and ¼ cup of the marshmallows.

5. Scrape the mixture into the prepared pan. Bake for 25 minutes, until barely set. Coat the top with the remainder of the marshmallows and bake for 5 more minutes. Set the pan on a rack to cool.

6. Cut into 1½- by 3-inch bars

Makes 24 brownies

What about the other Heavenly Hash?
In the sixties, vanilla ice cream studded with almonds and cherries was often labeled Heavenly Hash, and why not? It might have lacked chocolate, but it met all other criteria for being both hash and heavenly. The makers of Minute Tapioca even suggested a heavenly hash concoction of crushed pineapple, maraschino cherries, and Dream Whip.

Corned Beef Sundaes?
The 1966 *Woman's Day Encyclopedia of Cookery* (New York: Fawcett, 1966) offered a Heavenly Hash Parfait dotted with marshmallows, almonds, and candied cherries. It was listed right after Corned Beef Hash.

DESSERTS *on the* DIAL

Tapping the talents of the entertainment industry, Chunky recruited the lovable nerd Arnold Stang to proclaim that their candy bar was quite a "chunk-a-chaaw-clat." With an eerily similar inflection, Farfel the dog sang the theme "N-E-S-T-L-E-S . . . makes the very best, chaaw-clat."

CORNFLAKE MACAROONS

Crunchy on the outside, soft and gooey on the inside, these easy-to-make pecan, coconut, and cornflake meringues are more sophisticated than a lot of macaroons with fancy culinary pedigrees.

◆◆◆◆◆◆◆◆◆◆◆◆◆◆◆◆◆◆◆◆◆◆◆◆◆◆◆◆◆

4 large egg whites
Pinch of salt
Pinch of cream of tartar
1 cup sugar
1 teaspoon vanilla extract

1 cup pecan pieces, toasted (page 3)
1 cup unsweetened coconut flakes, toasted (page 3)
1 cup tightly packed cornflakes

◆◆◆◆◆◆◆◆◆◆◆◆◆◆◆◆◆◆◆◆◆◆◆◆◆◆◆◆◆

1. Set a rack in the middle and top third of the oven and preheat to 325°F.

2. In a completely clean, dry mixing bowl, with an electric mixer, whisk the egg whites, salt, and cream of tartar until very foamy and almost creamy. With the mixer still running, sprinkle in the sugar. Continue to whisk on high speed until fluffy, thick, and shiny. Whisk in the vanilla. Fold in the pecans, coconut, and cornflakes.

3. Drop walnut-size balls of batter onto nonstick or parchment-lined cookie sheets at 2-inch intervals. Bake for 15 minutes, turning the pans once, front to back, for even baking until lightly tanned and set on the surface. Set the cookie sheets on a rack to cool.

Makes 36 cookies

Cornflakes, like many other amorphous bundles, can be tricky to measure—a bit like trying to measure the Blob's waistline. Showing no mercy, firmly pack them into a measuring cup. It's fine if they smash. Just keep cramming them in until there's no more room and they fill the measuring receptacle.

CHINESE ALMOND COOKIES

As Chinese restaurants became the rage in the early fifties, so did the crumbly almond shortbread cookies that were served for dessert. The first rendition is said to have originated in a Chinese bakery in Los Angeles. Many versions contained secret ingredients like gin or vodka (try 1 tablespoon added in with the extracts). Most of them used lard and had an apricot kernel plopped in their centers. We substitute a combination of butter and vegetable shortening. You are, of course, welcome to spend an afternoon cracking apricot pits. But, if you have other plans, just go out and buy a sack of shelled almonds.

✦✦✦✦✦✦✦✦✦✦✦✦✦✦✦✦✦✦✦✦✦✦✦✦✦✦✦

2 cups all-purpose flour
½ cup white cornmeal
1¼ teaspoons baking powder
½ teaspoon salt
10 tablespoons (1¼ sticks) unsalted butter at room temperature
2 tablespoons vegetable shortening

1 cup sugar
1 large egg
1 tablespoon almond extract
½ teaspoon vanilla extract
1 large egg yolk
36 whole almonds

✦✦✦✦✦✦✦✦✦✦✦✦✦✦✦✦✦✦✦✦✦✦✦✦✦✦✦

1. Set 2 racks in the middle and upper third of the oven and preheat to 350°F.

2. In a medium bowl, stir together the flour, cornmeal, baking powder, and salt.

3. In a mixing bowl, with an electric mixer, beat the butter, shortening, and sugar for 15 seconds, until smooth. Add the egg, almond extract, and vanilla, and beat until fluffy, about 1 minute. Turn the mixer down to its lowest setting and gradually add the flour mixture, blending just to combine.

4. Drop walnut-size balls of dough onto nonstick or parchment-lined cookie sheets at 3-inch intervals. With moistened fingers, flatten the cookies out a little. Mix the egg yolk with 1 tablespoon of water to make a wash and paint a thin coat of it on the tops of the cookies. Press an almond into the center of each cookie. Bake for about 10 minutes, turning once for even baking, until the cookies are golden. Set the cookie sheets on a rack to cool.

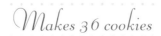

Makes 36 cookies

BLACK & WHITES

Hey, are these cookies or cakes? I have had some so moist that they fell apart when picked up. Others have been dry as crackers. The ideal should be light, moist, and buttery yet firm enough to handle. The pro bakers frosted with fondant, scooped and reworked out of giant buckets. We use a fondant-style glaze.

Black & Whites were sold at bakeries and delis all over the New York area but none could compare to the ones at Gotleib's in Brooklyn. Head baker Mernie Manheim was the kind of guy who could infuse magic into a cookie. We called his son, Larry, who let us in on the secret: "Hey, stick to the recipe and then add a lot of finesse."

Black & Whites had a resurgence when they were featured on an episode of Seinfeld. Will they, one day, achieve double retro status: "Can you remember back in the nineties, when Seinfeld used to reminisce about cookies from the sixties?"

✦✦✦✦✦✦✦✦✦✦✦✦✦✦✦✦✦✦✦✦✦✦✦✦✦✦✦

FOR THE COOKIES
2¼ cups all-purpose flour
1 teaspoon baking powder
¼ teaspoon salt
¾ cup (1½ sticks) unsalted butter at
    room temperature
1¼ cups sugar
3 large eggs
1 teaspoon vanilla extract
¼ teaspoon lemon extract
1½ cups milk

FOR THE FROSTING
½ cup water
½ cup light corn syrup
2 cups sugar
Pinch of cream of tartar
1 cup confectioners' sugar
1 teaspoon vanilla extract
2 tablespoons hot water
2 tablespoons unsweetened
    Dutch-processed cocoa
2 tablespoons hot brewed coffee

✦✦✦✦✦✦✦✦✦✦✦✦✦✦✦✦✦✦✦✦✦✦✦✦✦✦✦

1. Make the Cookies: Set 2 racks in the middle of the oven and preheat to 350°F.

2. In a medium bowl, stir together the flour, baking powder, and salt.

3. In a mixing bowl, with an electric mixer, beat the butter and sugar for 15 seconds, until smooth. Add the eggs, one at a time, beating until each is incorporated. Add the vanilla and lemon extracts and continue beating until fluffy, about 2 minutes.

4. With the mixer on its slowest setting, gradually beat in half of the flour mixture. Beat in the milk and then the remaining flour mixture.

continued

BLACK & WHITES, CHOW MIEN-NOODLE HAYSTACKS, AND CHOCOLATE SANDWICH COOKIES WITH VANILLA-CREAM FILLING

5. On nonstick or parchment-lined cookie sheets, drop ½-cup mounds of dough at 4-inch intervals. Bake the cookies for about 11 minutes, turning the pans once, front to back, for even baking, until the cookies are lightly tanned. Set the cookie sheets on a rack to cool.

6. Make the Frosting: Fit a heavy-bottomed saucepan with a candy thermometer. Over high heat, cook the water, corn syrup, sugar, and cream of tartar until it registers 240°F (soft ball).

7. Remove the pan from the heat. Vigorously whisk in the confectioners' sugar, vanilla, and hot water until creamy looking. Quickly spread half of the icing on one half of each cookie. Whisk the cocoa and hot coffee into the remaining icing. Spread it on the other halves of the cookies. Let set for 15 minutes.

Makes a dozen Big cookies

GINGERSNAPS

The gingersnap goes back to 1870, when the original prototype was baked at Pogen's bakery in Malmo, Sweden. This equally snappy version is even more lively, thanks to a jolt of fresh ginger. It is said that if you smash a gingersnap in your palm and it breaks into three pieces, good luck will surely come your way. Perhaps it would be better if a psychiatrist would come your way. What kind of a nut job goes around smashing cookies? Try eating these and good flavor will go right down your gullet. That's the way the cookie is supposed to crumble.

✦✦✦✦✦✦✦✦✦✦✦✦✦✦✦✦✦✦✦✦✦✦✦✦✦✦✦

One 2½-inch piece of fresh ginger, peeled
2 teaspoons ground ginger
2¼ cups all-purpose flour
1½ teaspoons baking powder
1 teaspoon baking soda
1 teaspoon ground cinnamon
¼ teaspoon ground cloves

¼ teaspoon salt
½ cup (1 stick) unsalted butter at room temperature
1 cup sugar plus a little for sprinkling
1 large egg
¼ cup molasses
1 teaspoon vanilla extract

✦✦✦✦✦✦✦✦✦✦✦✦✦✦✦✦✦✦✦✦✦✦✦✦✦✦✦

1. Set 2 racks in the middle and top third of the oven and preheat to 375°F.

2. Grate the fresh ginger with a box grater. Use the ground ginger to "mop up" any juice that has splattered around.

3. In a medium bowl, stir together the flour, baking powder, baking soda, cinnamon, cloves, and salt.

4. In the bowl of an electric mixer, beat the butter and sugar for 15 seconds, until smooth. Beat in the egg, molasses, vanilla, and ginger mixture until completely blended, about 1 minute. With the mixer on its lowest setting, gradually add the flour mixture, blending just to combine.

5. Drop tablespoons of the dough onto nonstick or parchment-lined cookie sheets at 2½-inch intervals. With moistened fingers, flatten and round out the cookies a little. Sprinkle them with a tiny bit of sugar. Bake for about 8 minutes, turning the pans once, front to back, for even baking, until the cookies are evenly browned. Set the cookie sheets on a rack to cool.

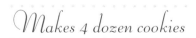

Makes 4 dozen cookies

CHOCOLATE SANDWICH COOKIES WITH VANILLA-CREAM FILLING

In 1912, Nabisco introduced three new products: the Veronese, the Mother Goose, and a chocolate sandwich that would become the world's most popular cookie. Today, five billion Oreos are sold in the United States annually.

Watch a group of kids eating them. They each have their own style. Some pull them apart and lick the filling. Others roll them against their teeth, scraping off layers of cookie. Then, of course, there are those who just have to dunk.

For one generation that grew up on Oreos, Sly Stone's message couldn't have made more sense: "Different strokes for different . . . cookies."

◆◆◆◆◆◆◆◆◆◆◆◆◆◆◆◆◆◆◆◆◆◆◆◆◆◆◆◆◆◆

FOR THE CHOCOLATE WAFERS

1¼ cups all-purpose flour

½ cup unsweetened Dutch-processed cocoa

1 teaspoon baking soda

¼ teaspoon baking powder

¼ teaspoon salt

1½ cups sugar

½ cup plus 2 tablespoons (1¼ sticks) unsalted butter at room temperature

1 large egg

FOR THE VANILLA-CREAM FILLING

¼ cup (½ stick) unsalted butter at room temperature

¼ cup vegetable shortening

2 cups confectioners' sugar

2 teaspoons vanilla extract

◆◆◆◆◆◆◆◆◆◆◆◆◆◆◆◆◆◆◆◆◆◆◆◆◆◆◆◆◆

1. Set 2 racks in the middle and upper third of the oven and preheat to 375°F.

2. Make the Chocolate Wafers: In a food processor or the bowl of an electric mixer, thoroughly mix together the flour, cocoa, baking soda, baking powder, salt, and sugar. While pulsing or on low speed, add the butter, then the egg. Process or beat until the dough is thoroughly blended and massed together.

3. Drop rounded teaspoons of batter onto nonstick or parchment-lined cookie sheets at 2-inch intervals. With moistened fingers, round out the cookies and flatten them a little. Bake for 9 minutes, turning the pans once for even baking, until the cookies are set. Set the cookie sheets on a rack to cool.

4. Make the Vanilla-Cream Filling: Put the butter and shortening in a mixing bowl and, at low speed, gradually beat in the confectioners' sugar and vanilla, until blended. Turn the mixer up to high and beat for 2 or 3 minutes more, until fluffy.

5. To Assemble: With a pastry bag fitted with a ½-inch tip, pipe teaspoon-size blobs of filling onto the tops of half the cookies. Keeping the smooth bottoms of the cookies facing up, flip the remaining cookies on top of the filling and lightly press to form sandwiches.

Makes 36 sandwich cookies

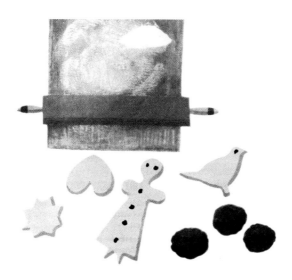

THE OVERSTUFFED SANDWICH COOKIE

Until Fig Newton's law of gravity (Scooter Pi r²) *buds in, there is nothing that will prevent you from doubling, tripling, or quintupling the stuffing in your cookies. By using mathematical calculations or bigger blobs of batter, you can also enlarge your cookies' circumference to make "jumbos."*

How about some new-fangled flavored fillings for your chocolate sandwich cookies? Just follow the directions for Vanilla-Cream Filling (page 148) and fill your cookies with . . .

◆◆◆◆◆◆◆◆◆◆◆◆◆◆◆◆◆◆◆◆◆◆◆◆◆◆◆◆◆

MINT CREAM FILLING
¼ cup (½ stick) unsalted butter at room
    temperature
¼ cup vegetable shortening
2 cups confectioners' sugar
2 tablespoons Peppermint Twist Sauce
    (page 194)
1 teaspoon mint extract

PEANUT BUTTER CREAM FILLING
1 cup creamy peanut butter (8 ounces)
1 cup confectioners' sugar
2 tablespoons unsalted butter at room
    temperature

◆◆◆◆◆◆◆◆◆◆◆◆◆◆◆◆◆◆◆◆◆◆◆◆◆◆◆◆◆

Here's another approach. Try these fillings stuffed in between Vanilla Wafers (page 156), Gingersnaps (page 147), or what have you.

THE DAGWOOD COOKIE SANDWICH

Mocha, peanut, jalepeño-anchovy—by now you've probably figured out that the sky's the limit. Freak out and fill your cookies with everything but the kitchen sink.

❖❖❖❖❖❖❖❖❖❖❖❖❖❖❖❖❖❖❖❖❖❖❖❖

1. Select the cookies of your choice: Chocolate Wafers (page 148), Vanilla Wafers (page 156), Gingersnaps (page 147), etc.

2. Pipe on your favorite fillings (pages 148 and 150): Vanilla, Peanut Butter, Mint. Or try jelly, jam, or preserves: grape, raspberry, even kumquat.

3. Alternate the fillings with sliced strawberries, kiwis, bananas, peaches, what have you.

4. Put it all together and what have you got? (See above for the correct answer.)

DESSERTS *on the* DIAL

On *The Joey Bishop Show*, Jillson's big weakness was . . . cinnamon buns.

FRIED-SPAGHETTI COOKIES

If you can imagine long, stringy miniature funnel cakes that are all crunch, then you've got Fried-Spaghetti Cookies.

❖❖❖❖❖❖❖❖❖❖❖❖❖❖❖❖❖❖❖❖❖❖❖❖❖❖❖❖

¼ pound thin spaghetti
Vegetable oil for frying

¼ cup confectioners' sugar
½ teaspoon ground cinnamon

❖❖❖❖❖❖❖❖❖❖❖❖❖❖❖❖❖❖❖❖❖❖❖❖❖❖❖❖

1. In a large pot of boiling water, cook the spaghetti until tender. Drain well, then toss with 1 teaspoon of vegetable oil to prevent sticking.

2. In a skillet or electric fryer, heat 1 inch of oil to 365°F. Working in batches of 3 or 4 tangled strands, fry the spaghetti until golden brown. Let the spaghetti intertwine to form interesting shapes. Drain on paper towels.

3. Set a rack in the middle of the oven and preheat to 350°F. Put the fried spaghetti on a cookie sheet and bake for 2 to 3 minutes, until evenly tanned but not dark.

4. Let cool to room temperature. Mix the confectioners' sugar and cinnamon together. Liberally dust on the cookies.

Makes about 2 dozen little bunches

CHOW MEIN-NOODLE HAYSTACKS

Digging up old recipes requires a bit of sleuthing, but having a good information source helps. Food writer, chocolate expert, and culinary stool pigeon Stephanie Banyas spilled the beans to me on chow mein–noodle cookies. As originally produced in her fourth-grade home economics class, they should be made with a combination of melted chocolate, butterscotch chips, and packaged noodles.

These are no rough-and-tumble Mickey Spillane–style noodle cookies. They are cool and sophisticated pasta confections, à la Peter Gunn. So, put some Henry Mancini on the hi-fi and get your spaghetti into hot water for a crunchy, chocolate caper.

❖❖❖❖❖❖❖❖❖❖❖❖❖❖❖❖❖❖❖❖❖❖❖❖❖

2 ounces spaghetti or 5 ounces packaged fried chow mein noodles

5 ounces semisweet or bittersweet chocolate

¼ cup unsweetened coconut flakes, toasted (page 3)

½ cup coarsely chopped unsalted roasted peanuts

❖❖❖❖❖❖❖❖❖❖❖❖❖❖❖❖❖❖❖❖❖❖❖❖❖

1. Boil and fry the spaghetti according to the instructions in Fried-Spaghetti Cookies (page 152, steps 1–2). Break the spaghetti or chow mein noodles into pieces no larger than 1 inch long.

2. In a completely dry bowl or in the top of a double boiler set over barely simmering water, melt the chocolate.

3. Mix in the noodles, coconut, and peanuts. Drop walnut-size haystacks of the mixture on a cookie sheet and refrigerate for 30 minutes to set. Serve chilled.

Makes 2 dozen cookies

VARIATIONS

For Rocky Road Chow Mein–Noodle Haystacks, stir in ¾ cup chopped marshmallows (⅓-inch pieces).

For White-Chocolate Chow Mein–Noodle Haystacks, substitute white chocolate for the semisweet chocolate and chopped pecans for the peanuts.

ANIMAL COOKIES

Animal crackers, or Barnum's Animals to be more exact, have been around since 1902. That was before cookies were even called cookies. We had not yet formally adapted the Dutch word kookje. *Their popularity has lasted through Marx Brothers movies, Shirley Temple songs, and the current change to endangered-species crackers. This recipe will hold shapes in three dimensions, so you can stamp out little critters with cookie molds. You may also use cookie cutters.*

◆◆◆◆◆◆◆◆◆◆◆◆◆◆◆◆◆◆◆◆◆◆◆◆◆◆◆

2 cups all-purpose flour
½ cup yellow corn flour* (do not substitute cornmeal)
¼ teaspoon baking soda
⅛ teaspoon salt
½ cup light brown sugar

½ cup (1 stick) unsalted butter at room temperature
2 tablespoons light corn syrup
¼ cup milk
1 teaspoon vanilla extract

◆◆◆◆◆◆◆◆◆◆◆◆◆◆◆◆◆◆◆◆◆◆◆◆◆◆◆

1. Set 2 racks in the middle and upper third of the oven and preheat to 350°F.

2. In a food processor or the bowl of an electric mixer, thoroughly mix together the all-purpose and corn flours, baking soda, salt, and brown sugar. On low speed, add the butter, then the corn syrup, milk, and vanilla. Process or beat until the dough is thoroughly blended and massed together.

3. Between sheets of wax paper, roll the dough to a thickness of ⅛ inch. Refrigerate for 30 minutes, until firm.

4. Cut the dough into animal shapes with cookie cutters or press molds (lightly floured to prevent sticking). Arrange on nonstick or parchment-lined cookie sheets and refrigerate for 15 minutes (this helps to maintain their shapes).

5. Bake for 7 minutes, until very lightly tanned around the edges. Set the pans on a rack to cool.

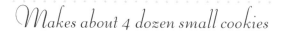
Makes about 4 dozen small cookies

*Corn flour is available in health food stores.

PECAN SHORTBREADS OR PECAN SANDIES

The Scots have shortbread and kilts. The French have sablés *and lingerie. On this side of the Atlantic, we've got Pecan Sandies and designer underpants. In 1955, the little elves at the Keebler Company looked under a cabbage leaf and discovered their first product of the same name. Keebler produces fifty billion cookies a year, but the buttery descendants of the French* sablé *are the pride and joy of the company. Fifty million Frenchmen and a bunch of elves can't be wrong.*

✦✦✦✦✦✦✦✦✦✦✦✦✦✦✦✦✦✦✦✦✦✦✦✦

1 cup pecan pieces, toasted (page 3)   1 large egg yolk
2 cups all-purpose flour   1 teaspoon dark rum
¾ cup sugar   1 teaspoon vanilla extract
1 cup (2 sticks) unsalted butter at room
    temperature

✦✦✦✦✦✦✦✦✦✦✦✦✦✦✦✦✦✦✦✦✦✦✦✦

1. Put the pecans, flour, and sugar in a food processor or a mixing bowl. On low speed, add the butter, then the egg yolk, rum, and vanilla. Mix just until the dough comes together.

2. Roll the dough between 2 sheets of wax paper to a thickness of ¼ inch. Refrigerate for 30 minutes, until firm.

3. Set 2 racks in the middle and upper third of the oven and preheat to 375°F.

4. Peel off the wax paper and cut out 1¼-inch rounds. Place them on nonstick or parchment-lined cookie sheets at 2½-inch intervals. Bake for 10 minutes, turning the pan once for even baking. The cookies are done when they are tanned around the edges. Set the cookie sheets on a rack to cool.

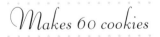

Makes 60 cookies

> For a real taste sensation, try substituting cashews, hazelnuts, or macadamias for the pecans.

VANILLA WAFERS

How can something so simple be so, so . . . ginchy. Don't expect the dense little chips that are sold in the grocery store. These cookies are crisp and tender. Vanilla wafers prove that homemade makes a really big difference.

◆◆◆◆◆◆◆◆◆◆◆◆◆◆◆◆◆◆◆◆◆◆◆◆◆◆◆◆◆

1¼ cups all-purpose flour
¼ cup cornstarch
1 teaspoon baking powder
½ teaspoon baking soda
¼ teaspoon salt
½ cup (1 stick) butter at room
    temperature

1 cup sugar
1 large egg
2 teaspoons vanilla extract
¼ teaspoon lemon extract

◆◆◆◆◆◆◆◆◆◆◆◆◆◆◆◆◆◆◆◆◆◆◆◆◆◆◆◆◆

1. Set 2 racks in the middle and upper third of the oven and preheat to 375°F.

2. Into a large bowl, sift the flour, cornstarch, baking powder, baking soda, and salt together—three times.

3. In a medium bowl, beat the butter and sugar for 2 minutes, until creamy. Beat in the egg and then the vanilla and lemon extracts until completely blended. With the mixer on its lowest setting, gradually add the flour mixture, blending just to combine.

4. Drop rounded teaspoons of dough on nonstick or parchment-lined cookie sheets at 2½-inch intervals. With moistened fingers, flatten and round out the cookies a little. Bake for 8 minutes, turning the pan once for even baking. The cookies are done when they are lightly browned around their edges. Set the cookie sheets on a rack to cool.

Makes 4 dozen cookies

*For the squares among us: Ed "Kookie" Byrnes's highest compliment was to refer to someone, or something, as being "ginchy." For example, "Baby, you're the ginchiest."

For Whom the
Ice Cream Bell Tolls

In 1960, Reuben Mattus opened American palates to a whole new world of richly flavored and textured ice cream. Reuben's marketing strategy was just as brilliant as his ice cream was yummy. Americans equated things that were European with luxury, sophistication, and an elegant lifestyle: Parisian fashion, continental dining, and music by Lawrence Welk. Get the picture? With a foreign-sounding name and a map on its lid, Häagen-Dazs appeared to come from some unknown northern European country, an imaginary land where skilled artisans have been churning fine ice cream for centuries. Of course, this was all fiction, and of course, Lawrence Welk was born and raised in . . . North Dakota.

French ice creams (as they are called in America) are made from crème anglaise, or custard sauce. Be an egghead and cook with care, especially when combining the hot ingredients with the yolks, a process called "tempering."

Ice Cream Tips

1. Ice cream machines may vary in price but most of them work perfectly well. Almost all of them are easy to operate.

2. A little sugar mixed in with the milk and cream will help prevent scorching.

3. Heat milk and cream just to the simmering point (it will wriggle in the pot). Add it to the eggs gradually, or you may end up with a scrambled mess.

4. Prevent your crème anglaise from curdling: Keep everything moving by constantly scraping the bottom of the pot with a wooden spoon. Don't overcook.

5. Cool down your crème anglaise in an ice bath to stop the cooking process. If it is slightly curdled, put it in a food processor and run on high for 30 seconds.

6. When your ice cream is ready, transfer it to the freezer so it can firm up and "ripen."

Ice Cream Bonbons

Are you behind the eight ball for a party idea? Serve your guests little cue balls of ice cream. Then let them dunk them into their favorite coatings. Set up small bowls of toasted coconut, chopped nuts, shaved chocolate, and, for ice cream truffles, cocoa.

Ice Cream Pies

An easy and fun-filled way to serve ice cream is to pack softened ice cream into a chilled crumb crust. For example: Del Monte's "Peach Party Pie" was pistachio ice cream in a chocolate wafer crust topped with canned sliced peaches. The food research department at Jell-O came up with "Easy-As-Pie Ice Cream Pie," which required no cooking and no freezing, and was "smooth and cut-able." All you had to do was blend ice cream with milk, beat in a package of instant pudding, pour it into a pie shell, and refrigerate for 1 hour. Suggested flavors—the usual suspects—chocolate, strawberry, pistachio, and, get this, lemon pudding—with pineapple ice cream.

Ice Cream Sandwiches

Instead of serving ice cream in the nude, dress it up. Put your scoops between two cookies and create instant ice cream sandwiches.

VANILLA ICE CREAM

Plain old vanilla—it's the most popular ice cream flavor in America, and when you get down to the nitty-gritty, there just ain't nothing like it. We've bolstered it up with a little brown sugar, which adds extra body and rather stylish substantiality (whew, what does that mean?). Always use pure vanilla extract; vanillin, the artificial stuff made from lumber, tastes like cheap perfume.

◆◆◆◆◆◆◆◆◆◆◆◆◆◆◆◆◆◆◆◆◆◆◆◆◆◆◆

1 vanilla bean
1½ cups milk
1½ cups heavy cream
1 cup lightly packed light brown sugar, divided

7 large egg yolks
1 teaspoon vanilla extract

◆◆◆◆◆◆◆◆◆◆◆◆◆◆◆◆◆◆◆◆◆◆◆◆◆◆◆

1. Split the vanilla bean lengthwise. Scrape out the seeds. Put the seeds, pod halves, milk, cream, and ¼ cup of the brown sugar in a heavy-bottomed medium saucepan. Bring just to the simmering point over low heat (it will wriggle in the pot).

2. In the meantime, combine the remaining ¾ cup brown sugar, egg yolks, and vanilla extract in a large bowl and whisk until just blended.

3. While gently whisking the yolks, drizzle the hot cream mixture into them so that they are gradually warmed up. Return everything to the saucepan and cook while stirring with a wooden spoon. Make sure that you are constantly scraping the spoon across the bottom of the pan so the custard does not scorch. The custard is done when it has thickened slightly and can evenly coat the back of the spoon. Do not let it come to a boil.

4. Strain the custard through a fine sieve. Press out all the liquid in the vanilla beans and nestle the container holding the custard into a large bowl of ice. Let cool, stirring occasionally.

5. Transfer the custard to an ice cream machine and freeze according to the manufacturer's instructions. Put the finished ice cream in a storage container and freeze until firm.

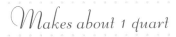

Makes about 1 quart

Now that you have this faboola homemade vanilla ice cream,
here are some nifty suggestions for what to do with it:

VANILLA FUDGE ICE CREAM

❖❖❖❖❖❖❖❖❖❖❖❖❖❖❖❖❖❖❖❖❖❖❖❖❖❖❖

¾ cup Chocolate Fudge Sauce (page 199)   1 recipe Vanilla Ice Cream (page 159) or
1 quart store-bought

❖❖❖❖❖❖❖❖❖❖❖❖❖❖❖❖❖❖❖❖❖❖❖❖❖❖❖

1. Set the fudge sauce in the refrigerator for at least 2 hours to thicken.

2. If the ice cream is very hard, let it soften in the refrigerator for 20 to 30 minutes.

3. Shmoosh and spread the fudge sauce in ribbons through the ice cream. Take care not to let the sauce blend into the ice cream. Refreeze until hard.

Second verse, same as the first...

BUTTERSCOTCH RIPPLE ICE CREAM

◆◆◆◆◆◆◆◆◆◆◆◆◆◆◆◆◆◆◆◆◆◆◆◆◆◆◆◆◆◆

Follow the procedure for making Vanilla Fudge Ice Cream (page 160). Substitute ½ cup Butterscotch Sauce (page 195). The sauce is sweet, so taste a little as you go and use sparingly.

With a cherry on the top . . . and more in the middle . . .

CHERRY VANILLA ICE CREAM

✦✦✦✦✦✦✦✦✦✦✦✦✦✦✦✦✦✦✦✦✦✦✦✦✦

½ pound Bing cherries
1 cup water
1 cup sugar

1 recipe Vanilla Ice Cream (page 159) or
1 quart store-bought

✦✦✦✦✦✦✦✦✦✦✦✦✦✦✦✦✦✦✦✦✦✦✦✦

1. Pit and split the cherries.

2. In a medium saucepan, bring the water, sugar, and cherries to a boil. Remove from the heat and let cool. Drain off the liquid and refrigerate the cherries.

3. If the ice cream is hard, let it soften in the refrigerator for 40 minutes until fairly soft.

4. Fold the cherries into the ice cream, then refreeze until hard.

> If you want to pit a cherry, then you need a contraption. They come in all shapes and sizes. I once had one that automatically set up and pitted 2 cherries at a time, then spat the pits into little buckets on the sides. Others look like loose-leaf hole punchers and can work just fine.

CHOCOLATE ICE CREAM FROM AN IMAGINARY EUROPEAN NATION

Are you looking for a nice light ice cream? Well, this is definitely not it! Ask any self-respecting chocoholic and they will tell you: Chocolate is supposed to be rich and deadly. Now, if a deep, dark, and intensely yummy chocolate ice cream is what you're seeking, then "Greetings, pilgrim, your search is ended."

❖❖❖❖❖❖❖❖❖❖❖❖❖❖❖❖❖❖❖❖❖❖❖❖❖❖

1 cup sugar, divided
1½ cups milk, divided
1½ cups heavy cream

1 cup unsweetened Dutch-processed cocoa
6 large egg yolks

❖❖❖❖❖❖❖❖❖❖❖❖❖❖❖❖❖❖❖❖❖❖❖❖❖❖

1. Combine ¼ cup of the sugar, ½ cup of the milk, and all of the cream in a heavy-bottomed medium saucepan. Bring just to the simmering point over low heat (it wriggles in the pot).

2. In the meantime, combine the remaining 1 cup of milk, ¾ cup of sugar, cocoa, and egg yolks in a large bowl and whisk until just blended.

3. While gently whisking the cocoa mixture, drizzle the hot cream mixture into it so that it is gradually warmed up. Return everything to the saucepan and cook while stirring with the whisk. Make sure that you are constantly scraping the whisk across the bottom of the pan so the custard does not scorch. The custard is done when it has thickened slightly and can evenly coat the back of a spoon. It takes about 2 minutes total, after everything is returned to the saucepan. Do not let it come to a boil.

4. Strain the custard through a fine sieve into a bowl and nestle it into a large bowl of ice. Let cool, stirring occasionally.

5. Transfer the custard to an ice cream machine and freeze according to the manufacturer's instructions. Put the finished ice cream in a storage container and freeze until firm.

Makes about 5 cups

*Y*ou can eat this ice cream in its natural state, straight out of the bucket (doesn't everyone?), but for a more complex dessert sensation . . .

Hey, Mrs. Tambourine Man,
turn, turn, turn that chocolate ice cream into a . . .

CHOCOLATE MARSHMALLOW SUNDAE

❖❖❖❖❖❖❖❖❖❖❖❖❖❖❖❖❖❖❖❖❖❖❖❖❖❖❖❖❖❖

Chocolate Ice Cream (page 163)
Marshmallow Fluff (page 198)
Chocolate Fudge Sauce (page 199)

Strawberries, (toasted) peanuts, pecans, walnuts, etc. (optional)

❖❖❖❖❖❖❖❖❖❖❖❖❖❖❖❖❖❖❖❖❖❖❖❖❖❖❖❖❖❖

This is a no-brainer: Just scoop (the ice cream) and goop (the fluff, fudge sauce, and nuts and berries).

Flaming Sundae

Any ice cream sundae can be turned into a burning spectacle. Soak a sugar cube in lemon extract or 151 rum. Press it into a marshmallow, place it on top of the sundae, and ignite. The burning sugar will even toast the marshmallow.

And now, for one of the most amazing chocolate concoctions of all time
(and the street named after Bullwinkle's buddy)...

ROCKY ROAD ICE CREAM

◆◆◆◆◆◆◆◆◆◆◆◆◆◆◆◆◆◆◆◆◆◆◆◆◆◆◆◆◆

1 cup stale Marshmallows (page 184) or packaged mini marshmallows
1 quart Chocolate Ice Cream (page 163)
½ cup chocolate chips

¾ cup coarsely chopped nuts (walnuts, pecans, cashews, hazels, peanuts, or any other of your favorites)

◆◆◆◆◆◆◆◆◆◆◆◆◆◆◆◆◆◆◆◆◆◆◆◆◆◆◆◆◆

1. With lightly floured scissors, cut the marshmallows into ½-inch chunks.

2. When the ice cream has just been made and is still soft, fold in the marshmallows, chocolate chips, and nuts. Transfer to a storage container and freeze until firm.

Makes enough to serve Boris, Natasha,
Mr. Peabody, and his boy Sherman

BUTTER PECAN
ICE CREAM

That rich flavor that says "butter" is really a combination of caramel and vanilla. (You can't believe it's not butter, eh?) If you're feeling adventurous, try a little substitution. You can use this recipe to make butter cashew or butter macadamia or . . .

◆◆◆◆◆◆◆◆◆◆◆◆◆◆◆◆◆◆◆◆◆◆◆◆◆◆◆◆◆

¾ cup pecan pieces
6 tablespoons water, divided
¾ cup sugar, divided
1½ cups milk

1½ cups heavy cream
7 large egg yolks
1½ teaspoons vanilla extract

◆◆◆◆◆◆◆◆◆◆◆◆◆◆◆◆◆◆◆◆◆◆◆◆◆◆◆◆◆

1. Put the pecans on a cookie sheet and roast them in a 350°F oven for 6 minutes, until fragrant, turning the sheet once, front to back, for even toasting. Set aside to cool.

2. Put 2 tablespoons of the water and ¼ cup of the sugar in a medium saucepan and cook over high heat until it turns to syrup. You may stir once to help dissolve the crystals. Continue to cook until the syrup turns a rich amber color. Stand back as far as possible and slowly drizzle the remaining 4 tablespoons of water into the caramel. It will bubble up and may splatter, so protect your hands with an oven mitt or towel. Swirling the sauce in the pan, cook for 2 to 3 minutes, until smooth and any solidified caramel has dissolved.

3. Carefully add the milk and cream to the pan and bring just to the simmering point (it will wriggle in the pot).

4. In the meantime, combine the remaining ½ cup sugar, egg yolks, and vanilla in a medium bowl and whisk until just blended.

5. While gently whisking the egg mixture, drizzle the hot cream mixture into it so that it is gradually warmed up. Return everything to the saucepan and cook while stirring with a wooden spoon. Make sure that you are constantly scraping the spoon across the bottom of the pan so the custard does not scorch. The custard is done when it has thickened slightly and can evenly coat the back of the spoon. It takes about 2 minutes total, after everything is returned to the saucepan. Do not let it come to a boil.

continued

6. Strain the custard through a fine sieve into a bowl and nestle it into a large bowl of ice. Let cool, stirring occasionally.

7. Transfer the custard to an ice cream machine and freeze according to the manufacturer's instructions. While still soft, fold in the pecans.

Makes about 1 quart

DANGER: Caramel burns! Use extreme caution.

DESSERTS *on the* DIAL

The Brady family treatment for tonsillitis—ice cream, of course.

ICE CREAM PARFAIT

From weddings to bar mitzvahs to annual luncheons for the Edsel sales staff, the parfait was the dessert to finish a fête with. Real parfaits, in the French sense, are nothing like these snazzy little sundaes. The name, however, was interpreted as "elegance in a tall glass": ice cream, chocolate sauce, raspberry sauce, and vivid green crème de menthe. The makers of Royal pudding even adopted the name for gelatin and fruit cocktail served in a tall goblet.

❖❖❖❖❖❖❖❖❖❖❖❖❖❖❖❖❖❖❖❖❖❖❖❖❖

1 quart Vanilla Ice Cream (page 159)
¼ cup Melba Sauce (page 124)
¼ cup Chocolate Fudge Sauce (page 199)
¼ cup Peppermint Twist Sauce (page 194)
1 recipe Whipped Cream (page 196)

FOR THE TOPPING
Nuts, chocolate shavings, chocolate sprinkles, fresh berries, maraschino cherries

❖❖❖❖❖❖❖❖❖❖❖❖❖❖❖❖❖❖❖❖❖❖❖❖

1. Scoop the ice cream and loosely pack the balls into 6-ounce parfait or wine glasses.

2. Drizzle the sauces down the insides of the glasses. Put on a thin rubber glove and press three fingers down the sides of the glass to create a marbled effect.

3. Top with Whipped Cream and your choice of topping.

Makes 6 to 8 servings

How the Sundae Got Its Name

Soda was first sold in pharmacies strictly for medicinal purposes, but in the late 1800s, ice cream sodas caught on as flavorific treats. Soda jerks had a heyday, inventing all sorts of concoctions. But, as with so many other enjoyable pastimes, self-appointed potentates of righteousness decided that they were far too much fun, and had them outlawed on Sundays. To get around these blue laws, the drugstores offered soda-less ice cream potions and sarcastically misspelled them *Sundae.*

BISCUIT TORTONI

In the days before chic Northern Italian dining, Mama and Papa ran the local Italian restaurant. For dessert they offered a bland slab of pastel ice cream called spumoni or a sensational frozen rum and cookie cream called biscuit tortoni. It was the original smoosh-in and had, long ago, been the rage of Paris. It was so successful that it drove its inventor, a guy named Veloni, into bankruptcy from overexpansion. One of his employees (yes, a guy named Tortoni) took the recipe and got his moniker on menus from Bangor to Boise. Now check this out, paisano: *You don't need an ice cream machine to make this dolce magnifico.*

❖❖❖❖❖❖❖❖❖❖❖❖❖❖❖❖❖❖❖❖❖❖❖❖❖❖❖❖❖

FOR THE ALMOND MACAROONS
4 ounces almond paste
½ teaspoon almond extract
½ cup confectioners' sugar
1 large egg white

FOR THE TORTONI CREAM
2 cups heavy cream
¼ cup confectioners' sugar
2 tablespoons dark rum
1 teaspoon vanilla extract
¼ cup almonds, toasted (page 3)
8 candied cherries (optional)

❖❖❖❖❖❖❖❖❖❖❖❖❖❖❖❖❖❖❖❖❖❖❖❖❖❖❖❖

1. Make the Almond Macaroons: Set a rack in the middle of the oven and preheat to 350°F.

2. In a mixing bowl, with an electric mixer, slowly beat the almond paste, extract, and confectioners' sugar until completely blended. Add the egg white and beat until smooth. Let the batter rest in the refrigerator for 15 minutes.

3. Spoon the batter into a pastry bag fitted with a ½-inch tip. Pipe out 1-inch mounds of the batter onto a parchment-lined or nonstick cookie sheet. Bake for 15 to 20 minutes, until puffed and tan. Set on a rack to cool.

4. When completely cool and crisp, chop the macaroons in a food processor. You should have approximately 1¼ cups of crumbs.

5. Make the Tortoni Cream: In a large bowl, mix together 1 cup of cream, the macaroon crumbs, and confectioners' sugar. Chill for 30 minutes. Mix in the rum and vanilla, and chill for another 30 minutes.

6. Whip the remaining 1 cup of cream to soft peaks. Fold in the macaroon mixture. Divide the mixture among eight 4-ounce paper cups. Top with the almonds and cherries, if desired. Freeze for 4 hours or until firm.

Makes eight 4-ounce tortoni

DESSERTS *on the* DIAL

They should have kept their day jobs. . . .

To earn a little extra cash, Robbie Douglas of *My Three Sons* set up a birthday cake business. Marcia Brady, on the other hand, worked in an ice cream shop. Lucy and Ethel got a short-lived job in a candy factory. They just couldn't keep up with the conveyor belt.

Sherbet

Once, on *Bewitched,* Darrin had to bring clients (and his boss, Larry) home for dinner. Samantha's father (played by Maurice Evans) convinced Darrin to woo them with a fancy-pants banquet from Chez Henri (complete with scantily clad waitresses . . . as if!). In the end, Samantha's down-home supper of chicken pot pie and store-bought lemon sherbet was what impressed them the most.

Traditional American milk sherbet is smooth, fruity, and a lot easier to make than the European egg white treatment. Many of our recipes call for half-and-half, but feel free to use whole or skimmed milk.

Any of these sherbets can be made into pops or bars with a mold kit. To make sherbet pops without a mold, pack your sherbet into 3-ounce paper or plastic cups. Insert an ice cream stick and freeze. When ready, just peel off the paper. You can also freeze mini pops in an ice cube tray. Remember that the process of scooping aerates and softens sherbets. Your pops and bars will be much firmer and possibly a bit icy.

ORANGE SHERBET

‹‹‹‹‹‹‹‹‹‹‹‹‹‹‹‹‹‹‹‹‹‹‹‹‹‹‹‹‹

1 quart orange juice
¾ cup sugar

1 cup half-and-half
½ teaspoon vanilla extract

‹‹‹‹‹‹‹‹‹‹‹‹‹‹‹‹‹‹‹‹‹‹‹‹‹‹‹‹‹

1. In a small saucepan, cook 1 cup of the orange juice and the sugar until the sugar crystals dissolve. Set aside to cool, then whisk in the remaining ingredients.

2. Transfer the mixture to an ice cream maker and freeze according to the manufacturer's instructions. Put the finished sherbet in a storage container and freeze until firm.

Makes about 6 cups

DESSERTS *on the* DIAL

Bobby Brady tried to impress his siblings by entering an ice cream eating contest.

LEMON SHERBET

1½ cups fresh lemon juice   ½ cup light cream
¾ cup sugar   ½ cup water
½ cup orange juice   ¼ teaspoon vanilla extract

1. In a small saucepan, cook the lemon juice and sugar until the sugar crystals dissolve. Set aside to cool, then whisk in all of the remaining ingredients.

2. Immediately transfer the mixture to an ice cream maker and freeze according to the manufacturer's instructions. Put the finished sherbet in a storage container and freeze until firm.

Makes a little less than 1 quart

PINEAPPLE SHERBET

◆◆◆◆◆◆◆◆◆◆◆◆◆◆◆◆◆◆◆◆◆◆◆◆◆◆◆◆◆◆

1 large ripe pineapple*　　　　　　　**1 cup half-and-half**
¾ cup sugar

◆◆◆◆◆◆◆◆◆◆◆◆◆◆◆◆◆◆◆◆◆◆◆◆◆◆◆◆◆◆

1. Peel and core the pineapple. Cut it into chunks and put it into a food processor with the sugar. Process until it looks like "crushed" pineapple.

2. Transfer the pineapple to a small saucepan and bring to a boil for 1 full minute. Set aside to cool, then whisk in the half-and-half.

3. Transfer the mixture to an ice cream maker and freeze according to the manufacturer's instructions. Put the finished sherbet in a storage container and freeze until firm.

Makes a little less than 1 quart

* For more information on pineapples, see pages 86 and 94.

STRAWBERRY SHERBET

❖❖❖❖❖❖❖❖❖❖❖❖❖❖❖❖❖❖❖❖❖❖❖❖❖❖❖❖❖

2 pints strawberries, washed and hulled   **1 cup half-and-half**
¾ cup sugar

❖❖❖❖❖❖❖❖❖❖❖❖❖❖❖❖❖❖❖❖❖❖❖❖❖❖❖❖❖

1. Put the strawberries and sugar into a food processor and puree until smooth. Mix in the half-and-half.

2. Transfer the mixture to an ice cream maker and freeze according to the manufacturer's instructions. Put the finished sherbet in a storage container and freeze until firm.

Makes about 1 quart

CHOCOLATE SHERBET

When you hear the bell on the Good Humor truck ringing, it's time for a very special chocolate sherbet called a Fudgsicle. This recipe makes a bucket that you can scoop, but feel free to make pops (see note on page 172).

❖❖❖❖❖❖❖❖❖❖❖❖❖❖❖❖❖❖❖❖❖❖❖❖❖❖

2 cups half-and-half
¾ cup water
1¼ cups sugar

1 cup unsweetened cocoa
2 tablespoons coffee liqueur, such as
**   Tia Maria or Kahlúa (optional)**

❖❖❖❖❖❖❖❖❖❖❖❖❖❖❖❖❖❖❖❖❖❖❖❖❖

1. In a small saucepan, bring the half-and-half, water, and sugar to a simmer. Remove from the heat and whisk in the cocoa and coffee liqueur, if desired, until completely dissolved. Strain, then set aside to cool.

2. Transfer to an ice cream maker and freeze according to the manufacturer's instructions. Put the finished sherbet in a storage container and freeze until firm.

Makes about 1 quart

Put 'em all together and what have you got?

RAINBOW SHERBET

. . . .

It's the old brick in a box, just like the artificially colored and flavored stuff from the supermarket. Only this time it's natural and tastes sensational. Mold your sherbets, then just slice and serve in lovely tricolored rectangles. It is most practical to make several blocks at once. You'll have enough on hand to feed the Little League team, a Shriners' convention, or a couple of teenagers.

◆◆◆◆◆◆◆◆◆◆◆◆◆◆◆◆◆◆◆◆◆◆◆◆◆◆◆◆◆◆

3 different flavors of sherbet (pages 174–177)

◆◆◆◆◆◆◆◆◆◆◆◆◆◆◆◆◆◆◆◆◆◆◆◆◆◆◆◆◆◆

1. Pour one of the sherbets a third of the way into one of the following: (a) a loaf pan lined with plastic wrap, (b) a plastic storage box from a Tupperware party or 99-cents store, or (c) last but not least (and probably best), an empty box of baby wipes.

2. Set in the freezer to harden a bit, then repeat the process with 2 more flavors. Freeze solid.

3. To remove, wrap a towel soaked in hot water around the container to loosen. Give it a shake and . . . *kerplop.*

SCOOPSICLES

The original Good Humor Creamsicle was a splendid vanilla pop coated in orange sherbet. Talk about refreshing! You can make a reasonable facsimile with two sets of ice cream pop molds. First fill smaller molds with the ice cream and freeze, then put these into larger molds and fill with orange sherbet. This is great for mass-producing fifty or sixty pops. If you want to make just a few, a more practical method goes like this . . .

✦✦✦✦✦✦✦✦✦✦✦✦✦✦✦✦✦✦✦✦✦✦✦✦✦✦✦✦✦

Orange Sherbet (page 173)   **Vanilla Ice Cream (page 159)**

✦✦✦✦✦✦✦✦✦✦✦✦✦✦✦✦✦✦✦✦✦✦✦✦✦✦✦✦✦

1. Freeze the sherbet in a 2-inch-deep pan. A cake pan will do fine.

2. Scoop a small ball of the Vanilla Ice Cream. Place it on top of the frozen sherbet, and while scooping, roll the ball to cover with the sherbet. The sherbet will wrap around the vanilla as you scoop. Serve as is, or impale it on an ice cream stick and freeze until hardened. Make as many of these scoopsicles as you want. Put the rest of the ice cream and sherbet back in the freezer for another time.

1 pint of ice cream plus 1 pint of sherbet will yield eight 4-ounce scoopsicles

Willy Wonka,
Eat Your Heart Out

*F*rom Loft's and Barricini's in the Northeast to See's out West, there once was a time when elegant candy shops dipped and molded their own chocolates, then packed them into adorable tins and boxes. Unfortunately, most of these places have performed disappearing acts.

Candy making has also become a lost art. It can be tricky at first, but once you have mastered an understanding of sugar syrups and the use of the thermometer it will become as easy as taking candy from a baby . . . Wait, that's not nice.

Slick Tricks for Candy Making

1. There are all sorts of manipulations and tests to determine the temperatures of sugar. The easiest one is to just invest in a good thermometer. It will probably run around $14. Always read it at eye level. As soon as you get it home, stick it in boiling water to make sure that it registers 212°F.

2. Be prepared and work quickly. Temperatures can rise suddenly and syrups can harden before you know it.

3. Store candies in airtight containers.

4. For easy cleanup, let pots soak in hot water. This will help dissolve any stuck-on syrup and gunk.

5. Avoid excessive and unnecessary frustration. Do not attempt candymaking on hot or humid days. When the weather is sticky, your candy will turn out even stickier.

WARNING: Caramel and other hot syrups can cause bad burns. Always stand back to avoid splatters. Protect your hands with a towel or oven mitt.

DESSERTS *on the* DIAL

Jeannie's favorite candy was something called a "pipchick." When Tony and Dr. Bellows tried them, they miraculously attained superhuman strengths. Tony begged Jeannie's mother for the recipe, but she sent him a fake, which put everyone on a freaked-out, bum trip.

AFTER-DINNER MINTS

There are two types of after-dinner mints in this world: One is a chalky little blob that is oftentimes filled with green or black tarlike jelly. Its habitat used to be oversized brandy snifters, the ones that are situated in between the toothpicks and the cash register. Now, in a serious bow to high tech, greasy spoons graciously present them in Plexiglas contraptions that clank them out, one by one, in a most sanitary fashion. We, however, are interested in the other after-dinner mint, the elegant little green or white disk with the creamy fondant texture that could turn any diner or dinner into a high-class eating extravaganza.

You may also adjust the strength of your mints by adding more extract. Some people like Altoids and others want it a little bit milder.

O.K., if you absolutely can't make the Peppermint Twist Sauce, you may make white mints by excluding it from the recipe.

❖❖❖❖❖❖❖❖❖❖❖❖❖❖❖❖❖❖❖❖❖❖❖❖❖❖❖❖

1 cup confectioners' sugar
¼ cup water
¼ cup light corn syrup
1 cup granulated sugar

⅛ teaspoon cream of tartar
¼ teaspoon mint oil or extract
2 tablespoons Peppermint Twist Sauce
(page 194)

❖❖❖❖❖❖❖❖❖❖❖❖❖❖❖❖❖❖❖❖❖❖❖❖❖❖❖❖

1. Sift the confectioners' sugar. Line a cookie sheet with baking parchment.

2. Fit a heavy-bottomed saucepan with a candy thermometer. Over high heat, cook the water, corn syrup, granulated sugar, and cream of tartar until it registers 240°F (soft ball). You may stir once to help dissolve the sugar crystals.

3. Remove the pan from the heat. Carefully whisk in the confectioners' sugar, mint oil, and Peppermint Twist Sauce. Drop teaspoon-sized rounds onto the cookie sheet. Let stand for 20 minutes.

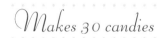
Makes 30 candies

MARSHMALLOWS

Pity the poor, humble marshmallow; overnight, it has been flung into the limelight. Now it is served with pride in the finest of restaurants. But it's not so off-base to bestow marshmallows with such patrician status. Their "roots" go back to ancient Egypt, where extracts made from the mallow root were reserved only for aristocrats. Marshmallows were the toast of nineteenth-century Paris and were accorded the same gourmet status as caviar or truffles. It wasn't until 1948, when gelatin powder and a high-compression method called "jet puffing" came along, that they could be mass-produced and toasted on open campfires by the proletariat. Without the benefits of a high-compression unit, homemade marshmallows may be a bit denser than the ones that you're used to, but wait until you taste them. They are simply scrumptious.

✦✦✦✦✦✦✦✦✦✦✦✦✦✦✦✦✦✦✦✦✦✦✦✦✦✦✦

All-purpose flour for dusting the pan
1 envelope gelatin (2½ teaspoons)
½ cup water, divided
½ cup light corn syrup, divided

¾ cup sugar
½ teaspoon vanilla extract
½ teaspoon dark rum

✦✦✦✦✦✦✦✦✦✦✦✦✦✦✦✦✦✦✦✦✦✦✦✦✦✦✦

1. Spread a ⅛-inch coating of all-purpose flour over 2 rimmed baking sheets.

2. In a small heat-proof bowl, soften the gelatin by stirring it into ¼ cup of the water. Set aside.

3. In a small saucepan fitted with a candy thermometer, bring the remaining ¼ cup of water, ¼ cup of the corn syrup, and the sugar to 240°F (soft ball). In the meantime, combine the remaining ¼ cup of corn syrup, vanilla, and rum in the bowl of an electric mixer ready with the whisk attachment.

4. Add the hot syrup to the mixing bowl and whisk at high speed for 3 to 5 minutes, until thickened. Set the bowl of softened gelatin over simmering water until the gelatin has dissolved, about 1 minute. Add the gelatin to the syrup and continue whisking for 6 more minutes, until white, fluffy, and stiffened.

5. Pipe 1-inch rounds of marshmallow onto the flour. They will spread a little, so leave room. The marshmallows will be set in 20 minutes. Marshmallows are sticky; dip your fingers in flour before handling. Before storing, make sure that they are dusted with flour so that they do not stick to each other. Before eating, dust off any excess flour.

Makes 24 marshmallows

Wanna leave out the rum? Well, that's just fine with me.

PECAN PRALINES

You say pray-leen and I say *prah-leen*.
You say *pee-can* and I say *pih-kahn*.
Pray-leen, prah-leen; pee-can, pih-kahn,
Let's cook the whole thing off.

First things first. The French have a hard-as-rock nut caramel that they call pralin. *This is not that. What this is, however, is the soft and delectable brown sugar candy that was originally conceived in New Orleans.*

◆◆◆◆◆◆◆◆◆◆◆◆◆◆◆◆◆◆◆◆◆◆◆◆◆◆◆◆

¼ cup heavy cream
¼ cup (½ stick) unsalted butter
1 cup plus 2 tablespoons (½ pound) light brown sugar

1 teaspoon vanilla extract
1 teaspoon bourbon
1 cup pecans, toasted (page 3)

◆◆◆◆◆◆◆◆◆◆◆◆◆◆◆◆◆◆◆◆◆◆◆◆◆◆◆◆

1. Line a cookie sheet with baking parchment.

2. Fit a heavy-bottomed saucepan with a candy thermometer. Over high heat, cook the cream, butter, and brown sugar to 240°F (soft ball). If necessary, stir once to help dissolve the sugar. Remove from the heat and let sit for 15 seconds.

3. Carefully (it may sputter) stir in the vanilla, bourbon, and toasted pecans. Vigorously stir with a spoon for 10 seconds, until the mixture looks creamy and slightly thickened. Drop by tablespoonfuls onto the prepared cookie sheet. Let cool for 20 minutes.

Makes 24 candies

CAUTION: The hot syrup may sputter, especially when the vanilla and bourbon are added, so stand back and protect your hands with a towel or oven mitt.

AFTER-DINNER MINTS, PECAN PRALINES, AND FRUIT & NUT SNOWBALLS

SOFT AND CHEWY CARAMELS

If you're looking for the kind of caramels that rip out fillings and stick to your teeth for hours, then sorry, Charley. These are soft and chewy, but they melt in your mouth, not in the dentist's chair.

◆◆◆◆◆◆◆◆◆◆◆◆◆◆◆◆◆◆◆◆◆◆◆◆◆◆◆◆◆

Nonstick vegetable spray
1 cup heavy cream, divided
¾ cup light corn syrup

½ cup (1 stick) unsalted butter
1 cup sugar
1 teaspoon vanilla extract

◆◆◆◆◆◆◆◆◆◆◆◆◆◆◆◆◆◆◆◆◆◆◆◆◆◆◆◆◆

1. Line a 9- by 9-inch or 7- by 11-inch baking pan with foil and lightly coat with nonstick vegetable spray.

2. Fit a heavy-bottomed saucepan with a candy thermometer. Over high heat, cook ¾ cup of the cream, the corn syrup, butter, and sugar to 246°F (firm ball); at this point the syrup will be golden. Remove from the heat and carefully swirl in the remaining ¼ cup of cream and the vanilla. Use caution; this is very hot stuff and it may splatter.

3. Pour the caramel into the prepared baking pan and put aside to set for 1 hour.

4. Lightly coat the blade of a sharp knife with nonstick vegetable spray. Cut the caramel into 1-inch squares and wrap in foil or cellophane.

Makes 6 dozen caramels

DANGER: Caramel burns! Protect your hands and face. Use extreme caution.

For extra-creamy caramels, swirl in ¼ cup sweetened condensed milk instead of the final ¼ of cream.

CARAMEL APPLES

Select a shiny red "out-of-hand" variety. That's apple lingo for good eatin' as opposed to cookin'. Mutsu, McIntosh, Fuji, and Red Delicious are all perfect choices.

◆◆◆◆◆◆◆◆◆◆◆◆◆◆◆◆◆◆◆◆◆◆◆◆◆◆◆◆◆

8 apples
1 recipe Soft and Chewy Caramels,
    cooked but not set (page 188)

1 cup chopped peanuts or other nuts of
    your choice

◆◆◆◆◆◆◆◆◆◆◆◆◆◆◆◆◆◆◆◆◆◆◆◆◆◆◆◆

1. Wash and completely dry the apples. Insert a stick into the stem end of each.

2. Prepare the caramel according to the instructions in step 2, page 188.

3. While the caramel is hot, dip and turn the apples into the caramel to coat and let the excess drip off. Dip the bottoms into the chopped nuts. Arrange the apples on a nonstick or wax paper–lined cookie sheet and let cool.

For a cute little hors d'oeuvre, dip and serve tiny lady apples. You'll have enough caramel to dunk up to 10 apples.

Popsicle sticks will work, but you can also buy rounded pointy sticks that are made just for candy apples.

RUM AND/OR BOURBON BALLS

It's belly-up-to-the-bar time for this waste-not, want-not chocolate confection. Bakeries used to make them with a hodgepodge mélange of ground-up cake trimmings. These stew-pendous little nuggets are perfect for teatime.

◆◆◆◆◆◆◆◆◆◆◆◆◆◆◆◆◆◆◆◆◆◆◆◆◆◆◆◆◆◆

8 ounces Vanilla Wafers (page 156), enough to make 2 cups
1 cup pecans, toasted (page 3)
½ cup unsweetened Dutch-processed cocoa, divided

1 cup confectioners' sugar, divided
¼ cup light corn syrup
¼ cup bourbon or dark rum

◆◆◆◆◆◆◆◆◆◆◆◆◆◆◆◆◆◆◆◆◆◆◆◆◆◆◆◆◆◆

1. In a food processor, chop the Vanilla Wafers into crumbs. Add the pecans and process just until they are finely chopped.

2. In a medium bowl, mix together the crumb-pecan mixture, ¼ cup of the cocoa, and ¾ cup of the confectioners' sugar. Add the corn syrup and bourbon or rum. Mix thoroughly.

3. Sift the remaining ¼ cup cocoa and ¼ cup confectioners' sugar onto a large plate. Form the crumb mixture into ¾-inch balls and roll them through the cocoa-sugar to coat. Store in a sealed container for up to 5 days. If necessary, touch them up with a light dusting of confectioners' sugar.

Makes 3 dozen

FRUIT & NUT SNOWBALLS

The traditional combination for this cookie/confection is apricot and walnut, but cherry, pineapple, and hazelnut proves to be a humdinger of a variation. By the way, this cookie requires no baking.

❖❖❖❖❖❖❖❖❖❖❖❖❖❖❖❖❖❖❖❖❖❖❖❖❖

½ pound mixed dried fruits (apricots, cherries, pineapple)

2½ cups unsweetened coconut flakes, toasted (page 3)

¾ cup coarsely chopped nuts (walnuts, hazelnuts, etc.)

¾ cup sweetened condensed milk

¾ cup confectioners' sugar, approximately, for coating

❖❖❖❖❖❖❖❖❖❖❖❖❖❖❖❖❖❖❖❖❖❖❖❖❖

1. Chop the dried fruit into ¼-inch pieces.

2. In a medium bowl, mix together the fruit, coconut, nuts, and sweetened condensed milk.

3. Sift the confectioners' sugar onto a large plate. Firmly form ¾-inch balls of the mixture and roll them through the sugar to completely coat.

Makes 36 snowballs

Sauces and Goops

ondering what to put . . . on top of old smokey? Everybody needs somebody, sometime. And sometimes, even the best of desserts needs a little sauce. Here are some suggestions for making your desserts a little more juicy.

Most of these sauces can be made in advance and stored in the refrigerator. Many of them can also be frozen. The best way to rewarm them is in a bath of hot water.

PEPPERMINT TWIST SAUCE

This brilliant green sauce is infused with zip and sock-it-to-me flavor. Who would have thought that anything so unadulterated could look so bright, so vivid, so Day-Glo. Is it phony? No, no, no. Use it to flavor after-dinner mints or to put some zing in an ice cream sundae. A little goes a long way, and it's all natural because "it's not nice to fool Mother Nature." This sauce has nothing to do with Joey Dee and the Starlighters or the Peppermint Lounge. You will, however, be thrilled at how much color and flavor you can literally "twist" out of those little mint leaves.

❖❖❖❖❖❖❖❖❖❖❖❖❖❖❖❖❖❖❖❖❖❖❖❖❖❖

¼ cup water
½ cup sugar

One 2-ounce bunch of fresh mint, leaves
picked and stems discarded

❖❖❖❖❖❖❖❖❖❖❖❖❖❖❖❖❖❖❖❖❖❖❖❖❖❖

1. In a small saucepan, boil the water and sugar until clear and all crystals are completely dissolved, about 3 minutes. Set aside to cool.

2. Dump the mint leaves into a pot of rapidly boiling water and cook for 1 minute. Quickly drain the leaves and plunge into a bowl of ice water. Drain and squeeze out any excess moisture.

3. In a blender, process the mint and syrup until smooth. Store in a sealed container. This sauce will keep for 3 weeks in the refrigerator or 3 months in the freezer.

Makes ½ cup

If you have some extra mint sauce left over, try flavoring some seltzer with it for a super-retro (back to the turn of the last century) soda called "peppermint get." It also makes a great sauce for ice cream.

Hint, hint: The sauce will be smoothest if it is reblended the next day when the mint leaves have softened up.

BUTTERSCOTCH SAUCE

Some butterscotch recipes call for brown sugar; others Scotch whiskey. We have two secret ingredients: Jamaican rum and sweetened condensed milk.

❖❖❖❖❖❖❖❖❖❖❖❖❖❖❖❖❖❖❖❖❖❖❖❖❖❖

¼ cup water

1 cup sugar

¼ cup (½ stick) unsweetened butter

1 cup heavy cream

1 tablespoon Jamaican dark rum

½ cup sweetened condensed milk

❖❖❖❖❖❖❖❖❖❖❖❖❖❖❖❖❖❖❖❖❖❖❖❖❖❖

1. Combine the water, sugar, and butter in a large saucepan and cook over high heat until light amber, about 5 minutes. Stand back as far as possible and slowly drizzle the cream into the caramel. It will bubble up and may splatter, so protect your hands with an oven mitt or towel. Add the rum and cook for 4 to 5 minutes, occasionally swirling the sauce around the pan, until thickened and a rich golden brown.

2. Strain the sauce and stir in the sweetened condensed milk. Store in a sealed container. This sauce will keep for 2 weeks in the refrigerator or 3 months in the freezer.

Makes 2 cups

WARNING: Caramel burns; use extreme caution.

WHIPPED CREAM

In the eighties, chefs demanded that whipped cream be served in a loose, runny plop called crème Chantilly. *Who did they think they were, the Big Bopper? In the good old days, whipped cream was presented as a hefty, free-standing glob—a voluptuous mountain that you could dig a spoon into. If you were lucky, it also had a cherry on top.*

◆◆◆◆◆◆◆◆◆◆◆◆◆◆◆◆◆◆◆◆◆◆◆◆◆◆◆◆◆

1 cup heavy cream
1 tablespoon confectioners' sugar

1 tablespoon maraschino, or 1 teaspoon
vanilla extract

◆◆◆◆◆◆◆◆◆◆◆◆◆◆◆◆◆◆◆◆◆◆◆◆◆◆◆◆◆

In a chilled bowl, whip the cream until slightly thickened, about 2 minutes. Add the sugar and maraschino or vanilla. Whip to soft, fluffy peaks, about 2 minutes.

CHOCOLATE WHIPPED CREAM

Use an electric mixer or hand whisk. Just make sure that the cream and all equipment are well chilled.

◆◆◆◆◆◆◆◆◆◆◆◆◆◆◆◆◆◆◆◆◆◆◆◆◆◆◆◆◆

½ cup confectioners' sugar
¼ cup unsweetened cocoa

2 cups heavy cream

◆◆◆◆◆◆◆◆◆◆◆◆◆◆◆◆◆◆◆◆◆◆◆◆◆◆◆◆◆

1. Sift the confectioners' sugar and cocoa onto a sheet of wax paper.

2. While whipping the cream, feed in the sugar-cocoa mixture. Whip to the consistency of shaving cream, about 4 minutes.

FUDGE SWIRL WHIPPED CREAM

❖❖❖❖❖❖❖❖❖❖❖❖❖❖❖❖❖❖❖❖❖❖❖❖❖❖❖

½ cup Chocolate Fudge Sauce (page 199)   Whipped Cream (page 196)

❖❖❖❖❖❖❖❖❖❖❖❖❖❖❖❖❖❖❖❖❖❖❖❖❖❖❖

In spoonfuls, drizzle the Chocolate Fudge Sauce into the Whipped Cream, then gently fold in with a rubber spatula so the fudge is streaked through the cream. Chill for 15 minutes to set before serving.

Maraschino is dark cherry liqueur with fabulous old-fashioned flavor. Do not confuse it with those bright red, pickled cherries.

Are You Haunted by Problem Whipped Cream????

Do you suffer from curdled, broken, or hard-to-manage whipped cream?

Does it have the consistency of California cottage cheese? The type that used to be served with green Jell-O and canned pineapple?

Here are some helpful hints:

1. Use a machine or whisk by hand, but . . . always use cold cream and chilled equipment (bowls, whisks, beaters).

2. Whipping cream works O.K. but heavy cream is richer and holds up much better. Ultra-pasteurized cream has a lot less flavor than either of the above.

3. Keep your eye on your target. Don't overwhip.

4. If your cream starts to break, add a little chilled cream to it and gently rewhisk until smoothed out.

FLUFFY MARSHMALLOW CREAM

Fluff is the glob with gusto. It tastes great everywhere, not just on fluffer-nutter sandwiches. Except for its color, Fluff has little to do with real marshmallows. It is, in reality, a form of cooked meringue. This recipe makes a lot, but it primarily consists of air. You'll want to keep a bucket in the fridge at all times.

◆◆◆◆◆◆◆◆◆◆◆◆◆◆◆◆◆◆◆◆◆◆◆◆◆◆◆◆◆

6 tablespoons water
1¼ cups light corn syrup
¾ cup plus 1 tablespoon sugar
4 large egg whites

Pinch of salt
Pinch of cream of tartar
2 teaspoons vanilla extract

◆◆◆◆◆◆◆◆◆◆◆◆◆◆◆◆◆◆◆◆◆◆◆◆◆◆◆◆◆

1. In a small saucepan fitted with a candy thermometer, bring the water, corn syrup, and ¾ cup sugar to 246°F (firm ball).

2. In the meantime, in a completely clean, dry mixing bowl, with an electric mixer, whisk the egg whites, salt, and cream of tartar until creamy and foamy, about 2 minutes. Still whisking, sprinkle in the remaining 1 tablespoon of sugar and continue to whisk until the whites hold very soft peaks, about 2 minutes. While mixing on slow speed, carefully drizzle in the hot syrup. Turn the mixer to high and whisk until thick, fluffy, and just warm, about 7 minutes. Turn the mixer to low and whisk in the vanilla.

Makes 5 cups

Order in the court 'cause here come da Fudge.

CHOCOLATE FUDGE SAUCE

❖❖❖❖❖❖❖❖❖❖❖❖❖❖❖❖❖❖❖❖❖❖❖❖❖❖❖❖

½ cup very hot brewed coffee

½ cup sugar

¾ cup unsweetened Dutch-processed cocoa

½ cup light corn syrup

4 ounces semisweet chocolate, chopped

2 tablespoons unsalted butter

❖❖❖❖❖❖❖❖❖❖❖❖❖❖❖❖❖❖❖❖❖❖❖❖❖❖❖❖

1. In a medium bowl, whisk together the coffee, sugar, and cocoa. Whisk in the corn syrup until all the sugar crystals are dissolved and the mixture is completely smooth.

2. Place the chocolate and butter in a large, dry bowl or in the top of a double boiler set over barely simmering water. When the chocolate has melted, whisk in the coffee-cocoa mixture until smooth and blended. The sauce is best if left to ripen for a full day before serving. Store in a sealed container. This sauce will keep for 3 weeks in the refrigerator or 3 months in the freezer.

Makes 2 cups

For Hot Fudge Sauce, place a heatproof container of sauce in a pan of hot water and set it over very low heat. Stir the sauce until warm.

RICH CHOCOLATE SYRUP

◆◆◆◆◆◆◆◆◆◆◆◆◆◆◆◆◆◆◆◆◆◆◆◆◆◆◆◆◆◆◆

8 ounces semisweet chocolate   **1 cup light corn syrup**
½ cup strong brewed coffee

◆◆◆◆◆◆◆◆◆◆◆◆◆◆◆◆◆◆◆◆◆◆◆◆◆◆◆◆◆◆◆

1. Finely chop the chocolate and put it in a medium bowl.

2. In a small saucepan, heat the coffee and corn syrup to a simmer. Pour the mixture over the chocolate and gently stir with a whisk until smooth and blended. Store in a sealed container. This syrup will keep for 4 weeks in the refrigerator or 6 months in the freezer.

Makes a little more than 2 cups

"Gee whiz!"

A Twenty-first-Century Retro Dessert...

HOT WHITE-CHOCOLATE FUDGE SAUCE

You can use this voluptuous and decadent sauce over ice cream, fresh fruit, or what have you. You can also double the recipe for a luscious white chocolate fondue.

❖❖❖❖❖❖❖❖❖❖❖❖❖❖❖❖❖❖❖❖❖❖❖❖❖

6 ounces white chocolate
¼ cup heavy cream
2 tablespoons light corn syrup

2 teaspoons dark rum and/or 1 teaspoon
**   framboise**
½ tablespoon unsalted butter

❖❖❖❖❖❖❖❖❖❖❖❖❖❖❖❖❖❖❖❖❖❖❖❖❖

1. In a completely dry bowl or the top of a double boiler set over barely simmering water, melt the chocolate halfway. Remove from the heat and stir to completely melt.

2. Combine the cream, corn syrup, rum and/or framboise in a small saucepan. Over medium heat, bring just to the simmering point. Pour the hot liquid over the melted chocolate and stir with a whisk until blended and smooth. Add the butter and whip for 1 full minute to thicken. Store in a sealed container. This sauce will keep for 2 weeks. To reheat, place a heatproof container of sauce in a bowl of hot running water and stir until warm.

Makes about 1 ¼ cups

HARD SAUCE

Quite oddly, Hard Sauce hardly looks like a sauce at all. A chilled little mound of it is served in a cute cut-glass dish and coupled with hot puddings, apple brown Betty, or even a warm piece of chocolate cake. When it comes in contact with something warm, it becomes happy and perky and bursting with flavor.

❖❖❖❖❖❖❖❖❖❖❖❖❖❖❖❖❖❖❖❖❖❖❖❖❖❖❖❖

½ cup (1 stick) unsalted butter at room temperature

1½ cups confectioners' sugar

Grated zest of 1 orange

1½ teaspoons vanilla extract

¼ cup brandy or bourbon

❖❖❖❖❖❖❖❖❖❖❖❖❖❖❖❖❖❖❖❖❖❖❖❖❖❖❖❖

1. In a mixing bowl, with an electric mixer, beat the butter, sugar, and orange zest until very light and creamy, about 6 minutes. Gradually, beat in the vanilla, then the brandy.

2. With a pastry bag filled with a ¾-inch star tip, pipe individual 1-ounce portions onto wax paper. Chill for at least 2 hours, then remove from the refrigerator 10 minutes before serving. (It should be served slightly chilled, not cold.)

Makes 1 ½ cups

VARIATIONS

Lemon Hard Sauce: Substitute the zest and juice of 1 lemon for the orange zest and brandy.

Brown Sugar Hard Sauce

✦✦✦✦✦✦✦✦✦✦✦✦✦✦✦✦✦✦✦✦✦✦✦✦✦✦

1 cup dark brown sugar
5 tablespoons unsalted butter at room temperature
¼ cup apple juice

1 teaspoon vanilla
2 teaspoons dark rum or applejack brandy

✦✦✦✦✦✦✦✦✦✦✦✦✦✦✦✦✦✦✦✦✦✦✦✦✦✦

1. Strain the brown sugar through a sieve to remove lumps. In a mixing bowl, with an electric mixer, beat the butter and brown sugar until very light and creamy, about 6 minutes. Beat in the apple juice, vanilla, and then the rum.
2. Pipe and chill (see step 2 of main recipe). Store in a sealed container. This sauce will keep for 2 weeks.

Makes 1 cup

INDEX

ice cream, vanilla, 159
    in bananas Foster, 114
    in cherries jubilee, 113
    in hot blueberry-lemon shortcakes . . . à la mode,
        80–81
    in peach Melba, 124–25
    in peach tarts, 54
    in pear tarts, 55
    in scoopsicles, 180
    in strawberries Romanoff, 117
    in tequila bandito mangoes and bananas Foster,
        116
I Dream of Jeannie, 26, 27, 182
I Love Lucy, 57, 171

Jack-o'-lantern cheesecakes, 28–29
Jell-O, 95, 104, 110, 158
jelly roll, raspberry-coconut, 21–23
Joey Bishop Show, The, 151
Joey Dee and the Starlighters, 194

Kabobs, fruit, 90–92
Keebler Company, 155
Kennedy, Jacqueline, 44
Key lime pie, 59
kirsch, in cherries jubilee, 113
Knox Gelatin Company, 59
Kraft, 104
Krebs, Maynard G., 82

La Crèmaillère, 111
La Rue, 111
lemon:
    bars, 137
    -berry gelatin, 107
    -blueberry shortcakes . . . à la mode, hot,
        80–81
    chiffon pie, 62
    hard sauce, 202
    pudding cake, 33
    sherbet, 174
Le Pavillon, 111
Lewis, Jerry, 133
lime:
    Key lime pie, 59
    -rickey angel food cake, 17
Lollobrigida, Gina, 2

Louise, Tina, 82
Lubin, Charles, 25

Macadamia shortbreads or macadamia sandies,
    155
macaroons:
    almond, in biscuit tortoni, 170–71
    cornflake, 142
MacMurray, Fred, 133
mangoes, tequila bandito, and bananas Foster,
    116
Manheim, Mernie and Larry, 144
Many Loves of Dobie Gillis, The, 82
maple syrup, in roast suckling pineapple, 94
maraschino:
    in cherries jubilee, 113
    in whipped cream, 196
marble cake, rum & cherry cola, 24–25
marshmallow(s), 184–85
    cream, fluffy, 198
    in bar-b-q-bobs, 92
    in crazy craters of the moon cake with moonrock
        topping, 7
    in heavenly hash brownies, 140–41
    in Honolulu hula-stick s'mores, 93
    in let's have a fondue party, 129–31
    in s'mores, 50–51
    sundae, chocolate, 164
    see also rocky road
Martin, Dean, 57
Martin, Mary, 133
Marx Brothers, 154
Mattus, Reuben, 157
measuring of ingredients, 4
Melba sauce, in peach Melba, 124–25
melon balls, towering inferno of, 88
meringue, Italian, in baked Alaska, 121–23
mint:
    cream filling, in the Dagwood cookie sandwich,
        151
    cream filling, in the overstuffed sandwich cookie,
        150
    peppermint twist sauce, 194
    white-chocolate grasshopper pie, 64–66
mints, after-dinner, 183
Minute Tapioca, 141
Mitchum, Robert, 26
mixers, electric, 5–6
My Three Sons, 133, 171